Vauxhall

Cavalier

All Cavalier models 1975 – 1979:

1300 L saloon, 1256 cc
1600 L and GL saloons, 1584 cc
1900 GL saloon, 1897 cc
Coupe and GLS, 1897 cc and 1979 cc
2000 GL saloon, 1979 cc
Sports Hatch GLS, 1584 cc and 1979 cc

Owner's Handbook/Servicing Guide

by Ian Coomber

ABCDE
FGHIJ
KLMN
PQR

Acknowledgements

Thanks are due to many people for their assistance to the author and publishers during the preparation of this Handbook, not least to Vauxhall Motors Ltd for the use of certain illustrations. Advice on lubrication was given by Castrol Ltd, and on spark plugs by the Champion Sparking Plug Company. Brian Horsfall carried out the various servicing operations, Les Brazier took the photographs and Matthew Minter edited the text.

A book in the Haynes Owner's Handbook/Servicing Guide Series.

© Haynes Publishing Group 1979

Printed and published by the Haynes Publishing Group, Sparkford, Yeovil, Somerset BA22 7JJ

ISBN 0 85696 432 8

Contents

Cavalier GLS Coupe

What's in it for You?

Whether you've bought this book yourself or had it given to you, the idea was probably the same in either case — to help you get the best out of your Vauxhaull Cavalier and perhaps to make your motoring a bit less of a drain on your hard-earned cash at the same time.

Garage labour charges can easily be several times your own hourly rate of pay, and usually form the main part of any servicing bill; but we'll help you avoid them by carrying out the routine services yourself. Even if you *don't* want to do the regular servicing, and prefer to leave it to your Vauxhall dealer, there are some things you should check regularly just to make sure that your car's not a danger to you on to anyone else on the road; we tell you what they are.

If you're about to start doing your own servicing (whether to cut costs or to be sure that it's done properly) we think you'll find the procedures described give an easy-to-follow introduction to what can be a very satisfying way of spending a few hours of your spare time.

We've included some tips that should save you some money when buying replacement parts and even while you're driving; there's a Chapter on cleaning and renovating your car, and another on fitting accessories.

Apart from the things every Cavalier owner needs to know to deal with mishaps like a puncture or a blown bulb, we've put together some Troubleshooter Charts to cover the more likely of the problems that can crop up with even the most carefully maintained car sooner or later.

There's also a set of conversion tables and a comprehensive alphabetical index to help you find your way round the book.

If the bug gets you, and you're keen to tackle some of the more advanced repair jobs on your car, then you'll need our Owner's Workshop Manual for the Vauxhall Cavalier which gives a step-by-step guide to all the repair and overhaul tasks on these cars, with plenty of illustrations to make things even clearer.

Cavalier 1300L saloon

Cavalier GL saloon

The Cavalier Family

The Vauxhall Cavalier was first introduced in October 1975 and its distinctive and rakish body styling was available in two-door or four-door saloon versions. For the more sports-minded a two-door Coupe model was also marketed.

Alternative power units at the time of introduction were 1584 cc or 1896 cc cam-in-head engines for the saloon models, the Coupe only being available with the larger engine.

Both saloon and Coupe models are well equipped, having heater, reversing lights and heater rear window as standard equipment. The Coupe also boasts a roll-over bar, an air spoiler and opening rear quarter lights. GL versions of the saloon have extras such as a clock, a glovebox light and a vanity mirror.

In 1967 the Coupe was re-named the GLS. Minor changes were made to the instrumentation on all models, and a driver's door mirror was fitted as standard throughout the range.

In October of 1977 the 1300 L model Cavalier was added to the range. This car uses the same 1256 cc ohv engine as that found in the Vauxhall Viva, and is otherwise the same as the 1600 L Cavalier.

The 1900 models were redesignated as 2000 in April 1978, the engine being increased in size to 1979 cc and modified to give improved performance. In September 1978 the GLS Coupe was joined by the Sports Hatch GLS; this latest version has a high-lifting tailgate and a folding rear seat, and is available with either the 1584 cc or the 1979 cc engine. A sun roof is available as an optional extra.

Specification details are given in *Vital Statistics,* but the following summary gives the most important changes to all models.

Vauxhall Cavalier

October 1975	Range introduced. 1584 cc or 1987 cc engines, 2-door or 4-door saloons or Coupe. GL saloon available with extra equipment.
October 1976	Coupe re-named GLS. Changes to instrumentation.
October 1977	1300 L model introduced with 1256 cc engine.
April 1978	1900 models re-named 2000, with engine size increased to 1979 cc and modified for improved performances. Gearbox and back axle ratios also changed.
September 1978	Sports Hatch GLS model introduced.

7

Road Test Data taken from **Autocar**

The figures published here are extracts from *Autocar* magazine road tests.

Fuel consumption: The mpg figure is the overall consumption figure for their test period, including performance testing. Many owners will achieve significantly better consumption figures. The formula on the right provides a guide ('**mpg**' refers to the quoted overall test figure).

Driving style	*Driving conditions*		
	severe −10%	average	easy +10%
Hard	**mpg** +10%	**mpg** +10%	+20%
Average		+20%	+30%
Gentle			

	Cavalier 1300 L	**Cavalier 1600 GL**	**Cavalier 2000 GLS**
Maximum speed (mph)	87	98	111
Overall fuel consumption (mpg)	30.9	27.2	25.6
Fuel consumption (mpg) at constant:			
30 mph	63.9	48.0	32.8
50 mph	44.8	41.0	34.8
70 mph	29.8	30.1	28.9
Range on full fuel tank (miles)	340	299	281
Acceleration (seconds):			
0–30 mph	4·8	3·9	3·0
0–40 mph	7·8	6·8	4·5
0–50 mph	12·0	10·0	6·6
0–60 mph	17·8	14·8	9·2
0–70 mph	28·3	20·0	13.3
Standing start ¼ mile	20·9	19·0	17.5
40–60 mph in normal top gear	15·8	13·0	9.6

These figures are copyright of *Autocar*, IPC Transport Press Limited. They are reproduced here with their permission.

In the Driving Seat

Having found out a few details of production history, let's take a look at some of the more important things that you'll need to know from inside the car. Fortunately, most things are straightforward for the experienced motorist, but a little more information on one or two points may be useful if you've just acquired your Cavalier or you're borrowing one from someone else.

Instruments and warning lights

The illustrations show typical instrument panel layouts which have been used on the various models. In general, they're self-explanatory, but the following points may help anyone who is not familiar with the car.

Ignition warning light

The ignition warning light indicates one of two things. First it reminds the driver that the ignition circuit's switched on (though the engine may not be running). Secondly it indicates that the charging circuit's inoperative and therefore in need of attention.

The ignition warning light should glow only when the ignition's switched on with the engine stopped, or when the engine's idling very slowly. As soon as the engine speed is increased to anything above idling speed the warning light should go out. If the light stays on with increased engine speed, then the charging circuit must be inspected as soon as possible, otherwise the battery will eventually lose its charge.

It's not advisable to leave the ignition switch in the 'on' position with the engine stopped, as apart from draining power from the battery, the ignition system wiring may overheat.

Oil pressure warning light or oil pressure gauge

When the ignition is first switched on the oil pressure warning light should glow, but as soon as the engine starts the light should go out and stay out. If it stays on, comes on when driving or possibly flickers at engine idling speed, this indicates that the engine oil pressure is dangerously low owing to lack of oil in the sump or mechanical wear or damage. Whatever the cause, if the light comes on or the gauge reading suddenly falls while you're driving, **switch off the engine and pull off the road as soon as is safely possible.** If the warning light came on to the accompaniment of loud knocking noises from the engine department, don't attempt to drive the car any further! Whatever the circumstances, investigate the cause of the oil light coming on and, if in doubt, don't run the engine again until expert assistance has been obtained.

As a guide, the oil pressure should not drop below 7 lbf/in^2 (0.5 kgf(cm^2) when the engine is idling at its normal operating temperature. When the engine speed is increased the reading should be over 28 lbf/in^2 (2.0 kgf/cm^2).

Temperature gauge

The temperature gauge won't operate unless the ignition's switched on. The gauge indicates the temperature of the coolant in the cooling system. Normally the needle should hover around the centre of the scale once the engine's warmed up. Should the needle stay in the 'cool' position after a few miles running, then this indicates that the thermostat in the cooling system is faulty and should be checked as soon as possible. If the needle moves into the red sector of the gauge then the coolant is approaching or has reached boiling point, and you should stop to investigate the cause. **Extra care must be taken when checking the coolant level if the engine's hot** – see *Filling Station Facts* for the right way to do it.

Voltmeter (when fitted)

Some models are equipped with a voltmeter which, as its name implies, registers the rise and fall in battery voltage. When starting, the indicator needle should not move into the red section of the gauge dial, and for normal driving the needle should be located between 12 and 16 in the black section. If the needle consistently indicates a low reading the electrical system must be checked for malfunction.

Tachometer (when fitted)

Only fitted to some models, the tachometer indicates the work rate of the engine in crankshaft revolutions per minute. The only thing to watch for on this is to ensure that the needle doesn't enter the orange sector; if it does, your right foot is suffering from an overdose of gravity and should be lifted!

Lighting and ignition switches

Most switches are self-explanatory in operation, but one or two peculiarities should be mentioned.

Lighting switch

This switch controls the sidelights, headlights and instrument panel lights. The switch positions are as follows:

O	Lights off
I	Side, tail, number plate and instrument lights
II	As position I, but headlights on as well

Combination column switch

The indicator signal lever on the steering column

The controls and instruments on a typical Cavalier

1	Handbrake lever	9	Face level ventilators	15	Instrument and warning lamps
2	Gear lever	10	Lighting switch	16	Heater controls
3	Cigar lighter	11	Heated rear window switch	17	Air booster switch
4	Ashtray	12	Indicator/wiper/washer/dipswitch stalk	18	Fuse box
5	Clock	13	Choke control (1256 cc engine model)	19	Accelerator pedal
6	Glovebox lid button	14	Horn	20	Brake pedal
7	Bonnet release lever			21	Clutch pedal
8	Side window defrosters				

Typical L and GL instrument panel

1 Indicator warning lamp
2 Clutch wear indicator lamp and/or handbrake warning lamp
3 Ignition lamp
4 Fuel gauge
5 Speedometer
6 Odometer
7 Temperature gauge
8 Oil pressure warning lamp
9 Hazard warning system indicator lamp
10 Main beam warning lamp

Typical GLS instrument panel

1 Tachometer (rev counter)
2 Speedometer
3 Temperature gauge
4 Fuel gauge
5 Voltmeter
6 Ignition lamp
7 Oil pressure gauge
8 Oil pressure warning lamp
9 Hazard warning system indicator lamp
10 Turn signal warning lamp
11 Odometer
12 Clutch wear indicator lamp and/or parking brake warning lamp
13 Main beam warning lamp

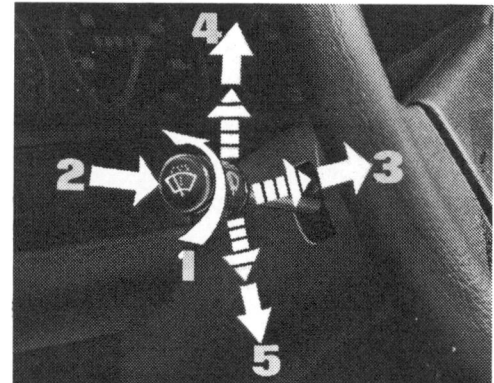

The combination switch positions

1 Windscreen wiper - twist knob to operate
2 Windscreen wash/wipe – push knob inwards to operate
3 Headlight beam control
4 Right turn indicator
5 Left turn indicator

The ignition switch/steering column lock

B Steering locked – ignition off
O Steering unlocked – ignition off
I Ignition on
II Start position

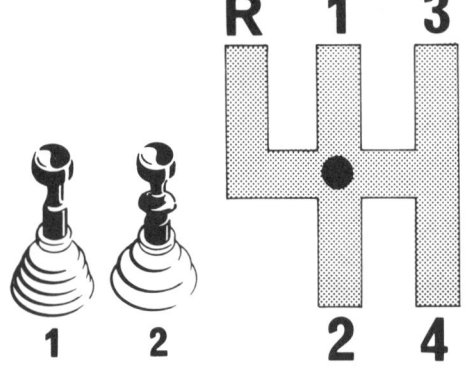

The manual transmission gear lever positions

On 1256 cc engine versions lift gear lever (1) to engage reverse. On larger engine versions, lift the collar on the lever (2) to engage reverse

also operates the windscreen wiper and washer controls, and also functions on the dipswitch. The various switch positions are explained in the illustration.

Combined ignition/starter switch and steering column lock

The switch shown in the accompanying illustrations and are as follows:

B – lock: When the key is in this position the ignition is off and the steering column is locked. The key can only be inserted or extracted from the switch when in this position. If the key should prove reluctant to be removed, move the steering wheel to the right and left whilst pulling on the key. **Note:** *Never leave the key in this position when being towed or when the vehicle is in motion!*

0 – Ignition off: The ignition is still off but the steering column lock is released. Use this position when being towed.

I – Ignition on: In this position the ignition is on and the steering lock is inoperative. The ignition and oil pressure warning lights will glow in this position when the engine is not running.

II – Start: The key is turned to this position to operate the starter motor. As soon as the engine fires the key should be released, when it will return automatically to position I.

Keys

Loss of the ignition key can prove rather inconvenient and sometimes embarassing! There are no lock serial numbers on the lock barrels, for security reasons, so unless you know the key number you're in trouble! Even knowing the number does not necessarily mean that you'll be able to get an over-the-counter replacement, so it's a good idea to always carry a spare ignition key with you (not in the car!) or at least record the number for emergency use.

Choke controls

Manual choke

On models fitted with a manual choke, the operating knob will be found on the lower facia panel, to the left of the steering column. This knob should only be operated when the engine is cold. Pull the knob fully out when starting from cold; when the engine is running push it progressively in until the engine will idle without it. A fast idle choke setting is available by pulling the knob out about $\frac{1}{2}$ inch (12 mm), but don't leave it in this position.

Automatic choke

On vehicles equipped with an automatic choke control the starting procedure is as follows. With a cold engine, fully depress the throttle pedal to the floor and release it. This action will set the automatic choke control and fast idle according to the air and engine temperatures. Operate the starter and when the engine is running increase the idle speed a fraction by slightly pressing down on the throttle pedal and then releasing it. The automatic choke will then increase the idle speed until the engine temperature rises, when the idle speed will progressively drop. At the normal engine operating temperature the recommended idle speed will be reached.

If the engine is warm when starting, press the throttle pedal half way down and operate the starter.

If the engine is at its normal operating temperature the engine should start without using the throttle pedal, but it may be necessary to completely press down the pedal. The accelerator pedal must now be continuously pumped when starting the engine as this will cause it to flood and prevent it from firing. To clear a suspected flooded engine, hold down the throttle pedal and operate the starter at the same time.

On automatic transmission models the fast idle when the engine is cold will cause the car to 'creep' when the selector lever is being moved to a driving position. The footbrake or handbrake should therefore be applied during this period.

Manual transmission

The operation of the manual transmission is conventional and simple, there being synchromesh on all forward gears. However, one point worthy of mention is the reverse gear engagement. On 1300 models the gear lever is pulled upwards before engaging reverse gear. On larger engined models the lever has a collar below the knob which must be lifted before reverse gear is engaged. This is necessary to prevent reverse gear accidentally being engaged, which could be both embarassing and expensive!

Automatic transmission

Automatic transmission is available on 1600, 1900 and 2000 models. The transmission comprises a hydraulic torque converter, which increases the engine torque according to the operating conditions, and a hydraulically controlled transmission giving three forward gears and one reverse gear. The gear changes are fully automatic and dependent on the road speed and throttle pedal pressure.

The respective selector positions are shown in the accompanying illustration. As with most automatic gearboxes there is an inhibitor switch which prevents engine starting in any selector positions other than P or N.

When selecting a gear when the car is stationary, **13**

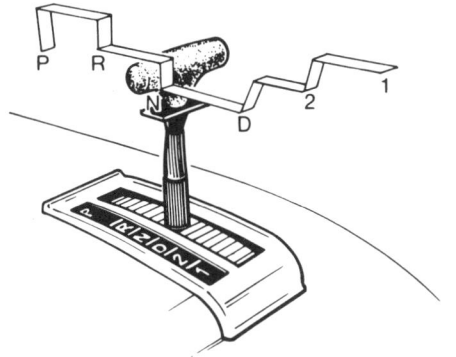

The automatic transmission selector

P   *Park*
R   *Reverse*
N   *Neutral*
D   *Drive (forward)*
2   *Intermediate*
I   *Low*

ensure that the handbrake or footbrake is fully applied and the idle speed is normal – don't race the engine. The operation of the various selector positions is as follows:

P (Park): In this position whether the engine is stopped or running, no gears are engaged, and the transmission is effectively locked. Although the engine may be started, the car cannot be moved in this position. When selecting P the car must always be stationary or damage will result. Engage this position when making adjustments or tuning the engine.

R (Reverse): In this position reverse gear is engaged. It is necessary to raise the selector lever collar to move the lever into this position. Never engage this gear when the car is moving forwards. A fast idle is useful in this gear to induce 'creep' for easy control when parking or manoeuvring.

N (Neutral): The same as P, except that the transmission is unlocked. The car can therefore be towed in this position, but not too far or too fast – see *In an Emergency.* The engine may be started in this position.

D (Drive): This is the selector position for normal driving. All gear changes are fully automatic and gear selection is dependent on the road speed and throttle position.

2 (Intermediate): This gear can only be selected after lifting the collar on the selector lever. This gear is particularly useful for engine braking, such as when descending steep hills. When selected, the transmission will operate as in D, but no change up to top gear will occur.

1 (Low): This gear also can only be selected after lifting the selector lever collar. When selected, no automatic change up will take place and this gear

is therefore particularly useful for engine braking on steep hills, especially when towing. Never change into this gear from D or 2 at high speeds – only at a speed within its range (up to 30 mph or 50 km/h).

Control techniques

Creep: This will occur when a gear's engaged and the engine idling, once the handbrake's released. It can be very useful when manoeuvring in confined spaces, and will be more noticeable when the engine's cold and the choke's in operation resulting in a faster engine idling speed.

Winter starting: The transmission will warm up and be more responsive if the car's driven with 2 (intermediate gear) selected and held for a few hundred yards before D is selected.

Steep gradients: When descending steep hills, a greater degree of engine braking can be achieved if 1 (low gear) or 2 (intermediate gear) is selected. The general rule applies that if the gradient's shallow or there's a succession of hairpin bends 2 (intermediate gear) should be selected; if, however, the gradient's very steep select 1 (low gear) for maximum engine braking. When climbing steep gradients, the transmission will change down automatically, there's no need to select low gear manually.

Kickdowns: If you push the throttle pedal to the floor, upward gear changes will take place at the highest possible speeds; if you're in top or intermediate gear, the transmission will change down if speed isn't too high for the gear below, thus giving you even better acceleration. This can be very useful when maximum acceleration is required, but if you make a habit of it you must expect your fuel consumption to suffer.

Filling Station Facts

Forgetting about the actual servicing and mechanical maintenance of your car for the time being, there are some things which are so simple they're likely to get overlooked; but they're not only an important part of the maintenance of your car – they're vital for its safety and reliability too. Three of these items – tyres, oil and water – you can check if necessary whenever you visit a petrol station.

We've set out here the absolute minimum of information you need right from the very first day you drive a Cavalier.

Topping-up oil

Whenever you top-up the oil level, always try to use the same grade and brand; and do avoid using cheap oil – the initial saving will probably be lost in increased engine wear over a prolonged period – or perhaps a short one!

When checking the oil level, ensure that the car's standing on level ground. Take out the dipstick, wipe it clean, then replace it fully. Pull it out again and note the oil level. Under no circumstances should the level be allowed to drop below the ADD OIL mark. If the oil level is at this mark, top-up the recommended grade to bring the level up to the full mark, but don't overfill! 1300 Cavaliers need about 2 pints (1.14 litres) of oil to bring the level up from the low mark to the FULL line on the dipstick; all the larger engined models need about $2\frac{1}{2}$ pints (1.5 litres).

Checking coolant level

If the engine's at its normal running temperature or higher, **take extra care** when removing the radiator filler cap. Place a rag over the cap, turn

Topping-up with oil

The radiator filler cap

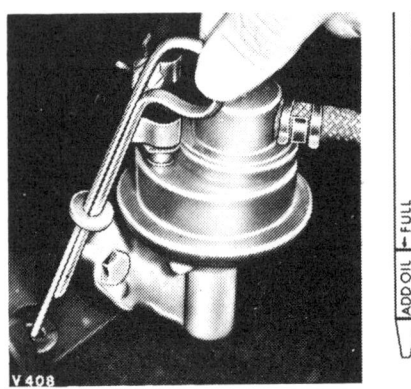

ADD OIL ← FULL

The dipstick is on the right-hand side of the engine

slowly anti-clockwise to the first position, and allow the pressure in the system to escape, then again turn anti-clockwise and remove carefully.

If a considerable amount of water's required to top-up or you're continuously adding water during the winter months, the antifreeze mixture will be diluted and made less effective. So if antifreeze is in use, topping-up should be done with water/antifreeze mixture in the correct proportions.

The coolant level should be brought up to 1 inch (25 mm) below the bottom of the filler neck. Make sure that the radiator cap's properly fitted afterwards.

Tyre pressures

When checking tyre pressures don't forget to check the pressure in the spare – in the event of a puncture you could be in for a 'let down'! If you're affluent enough to have your own tyre pressure gauge, always use this to check the pressures – garage gauges aren't always accurate and it's essential that the pressures are right to ensure the correct handling of the car when steering and braking.

Remember that tyre pressures can only be checked accurately when the tyres are cold. Any tyre that's travelled more than a mile or so will show a pressure increase of several pounds per square inch— maybe more than 5 lbf/in^2 after a long run. So a certain amount of 'guesstimation' comes into checking tyres if they're warm.

Since the pressures won't increase for any reason other than heat, the least you can do is to ensure that the pressures in the two front tyres are equal, bearing in mind that they may be a bit above those shown in the table. (The same applies to the two back tyres, but remember that their pressure may be different from the front).

If one tyre of a pair has a low pressure when hot, bring it up to the pressure of the other at the same end of the car; if they're both below the recommended cold pressures although warm, the safest thing to do is to bring them up to about 3 lbf/in^2 above it, to allow for cooling.

Self-service garages

Many garages now operate on a self-service basis so that the customer's subjected to the intricacies of refuelling his or her own vehicle. Regulars to this type of establishment need no introduction to its methods of operation and can usually be seen going through the routine at high speed like well-oiled robots. To the newcomer, the operation of the various kinds of pump can at first be confusing, but don't panic! Carefully read each instruction on the pump in turn before attempting to work it. When refuelling, insert the nozzle fully into the car's filler tube and try to regulate the fuel flow at an even rate so that it's not too fast. Most pumps now have an automatic flow-back valve mechanism fitted in them, which prevents any surplus petrol making a speedy exit from the filler neck all over the unsuspecting operator. On completion, don't forget to refit your petrol filler cap!

QUICK-CHECK CHART

TYRE PRESSURES

Recommended pressures for cold tyres in lbf/in^2 (kgf/cm^2)

	Normal		*Full load*	
Tyre size	*Front*	*Rear*	*Front*	*Rear*
165SR 13 (Saloon)	24 (1.65)	24 (1.65)	29 (2.0)	32 (2.2)
185/70HR 13 (Coupe)	26 (1.8)	26 (1.8)	29 (2.0)	29 (2.0)

FUEL OCTANE RATING
All models

97 octane minimum (4 star)

FUEL TANK CAPACITY
Early 1300 models
All other models

8 gallons (36.4 litres)
11 gallons (50.0 litres)

ENGINE OIL GRADE
All models

Multigrade 20W/50

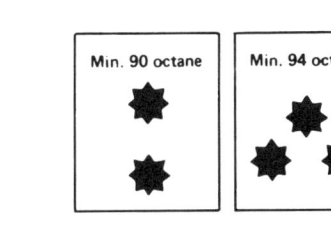  

Fuel octane/star ratings. Use the correct grade for your model

In an Emergency

There's been no car yet invented that can guarantee you a safe and reliable journey from A to B every day of your life. Whether it's due to a puncture or a more serious mechanical problem, the time will almost certainly come when your trusty transport needs a bit of roadside attention. The Troubleshooter section should help to trace the cause of an unexpected fault, but it isn't much good knowing what's wrong if you've nothing to put it right with, or needing to change a wheel in the dark when you haven't a clue how the jack works. A few minutes spent reading through this section now could save you much time and temper later on!

Spares and repairs kit

The basic tools supplied with the car won't get you very far in the event of a roadside breakdown. An additional tool kit is essential if you're to hope to carry out any repairs yourself — and anyway, you'll need them eventually for servicing; there's more information on the sort of items to buy in *Tools for the Job*.

A few things which can be fitted without too much bother at the roadside should also be carried. It's really up to you to decide what sort of repairs are within your capabilities in an emergency, but the kind of things you should consider are:

    Spark plug, clean and with the correct gap
    HT lead and plug cap — long enough to reach the plug furthest from the distributor
    Set of main light bulbs
    Tyre pressure gauge
    Spare fuses
    Distributor rotor, condenser and contact points
    Fan belt
    Roll of insulating tape
    Tin of radiator sealer and a hose bandage
    Extension light and lead with crocodile clips, or a good torch
    Clean lint-free cloth
    Breakdown triangle
    Tow rope
    First aid box
    Spare set of keys (but not kept in the car)
    De-icer aerosol (during winter)
    This Handbook or Haynes Workshop Manual

Of course, it's possible to expand this list indefinitely; for example, you might prefer to have a set of spare coolant hoses instead of just a repair bandage, but obviously there has to be a compromise or you'll have no spare room in the boot!

We'll mention here just three other items for emergency use which it might make you feel happier to have on board. The first is a 'universal' temporary fan belt which can be fitted without loosening any bolts, and which will enable you to get going again quickly in the event of a belt breakage, and fit a

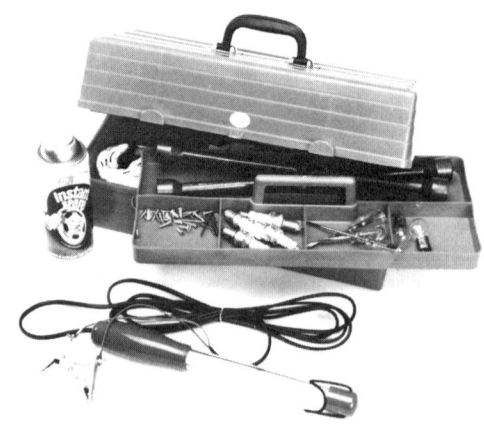

A box like this is useful for keeping your emergency repairs kit together

If you want to carry emergency petrol, use an approved safety can of the type shown here. The detachable spout makes pouring easy, too

An 'Instant Spare' aerosol in use on a flat tyre

proper replacement belt at your leisure.

The second 'get-you-home' device is an 'instant' puncture repair in the form of an aerosol can. The nozzle is screwed on to the tyre valve, and releases sealant to seal the leak, together with gas to reinflate the tyre. It's suitable for tubed or tubeless tyres, and will at the very least allow you to drive to a garage without getting your hands dirty.

Our third additional suggestion is a temporary windscreen. If you've ever suffered a shattered screen, you'll know what a nightmare it c n be trying to drive the car, especially in bad we t' er. If you haven't, take our word for it!

One of the roll-up type of polyeste emporary screens is quick and easy to fit, le s driving unaffected, and wipers and washers can be used normally. When not in use its thin container stows neatly in a corner of the boot or on the back shelf.

If you want to carry a spare gallon of petrol in the boot for emergencies, use one of the special cans made for the purpose. They're designed to be safe in case of an accident, and are much easier to pour from than an old oil can.

Another item well worth carrying is an aerosol can of ignition waterproofer which is particularly beneficial on damp mornings or when motorway spray and rain get into your ignition system. If the car fails to start or misfires under these conditions, a quick squirt applied to the coil, ignition leads and distributor cap will chase off any moisture present and save much time and aggravation drying and cleaning the various individual components.

Jacking up and changing a wheel

However, even the most carefully looked-after car will let you down some day. Punctures are still a common event, and although changing a wheel isn't the major operation it used to be, it's still not a pastime to be recommended, especially as it always seems to need doing on a cold wet night; and you won't feel any better with your spouse or mother-in-law looking on in scorn as you discover that the spare's flat and you've no idea how the jack works. If you're not familiar with the jack supplied with your Cavalier, read on – because one day you're going to need to use it!

Whenever the car's to be jacked up (either to change a wheel or for any other purpose) the car must be parked on firm, flat ground. The jack supplied with the vehicle is intended only for raising the car in the event of a puncture to change the wheel. It shouldn't be used to lift the car to perform any major tasks underneath unless it is further supported with chassis **19**

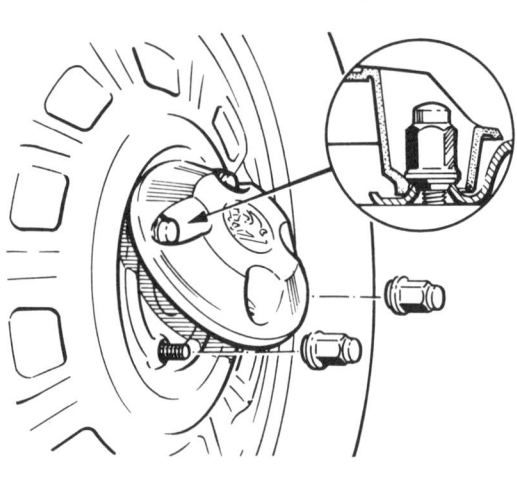

An emergency windscreen is fitted in seconds and can save untold discomfort

The GL and GLS model centre wheel insert. Remove
at least two wheel nuts before detaching the insert

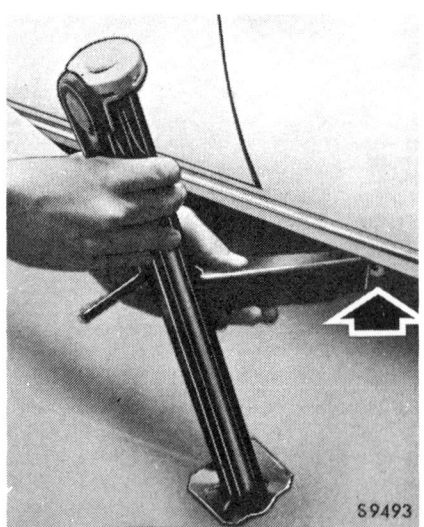

Inserting the jack lifting arm into a jacking point

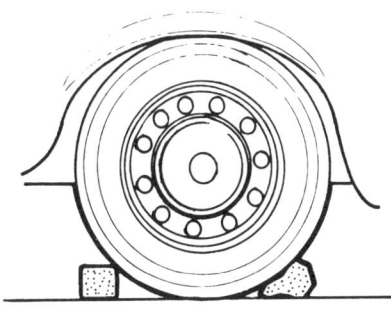

Always wedge the wheels before jacking

stands or blocks to make it secure.

The spare wheel, jack and wheel nut spanner are carried in the boot; the jack and the spanner are stowed behind the spare wheel, which is strapped in.

If a wheel is to be changed at the roadside, switch on your hazard warning lights if necessary to warn others of your predicament. Prior to jacking up, check that you have fully applied the handbrake and engaged first gear. If available, place a block or a large stone each side of the wheel diagonally opposite the wheel being changed.

The wheel nut spanner has a specially designed blade on its end and this is used as a lever to remove the hub plate from the wheel. Insert the blade between the wheel and hub plate, position the socket end of the spanner against the tyre, and tap the socket end to spring the hub plate free. To avoid scratching the hub plate place a piece of rag on the ground for it to land on. Some GL and GLS variants are fitted with a centre insert as shown in the illustration, and on this type the wheel nuts are already exposed.

Unscrew each wheel nut about half a turn. If the nuts are reluctant to move under hand pressure, try using your foot on the spanner, but take care that the spanner doesn't suddenly slip off the nut.

The jack can now be placed in position. There are four jacking points provided, two on each side below the door sill, one just forward of the rear wheel arch and the other just to the rear of the front wheel arch. Slide the jack lifting arm fully into position up to its stop, and angle the jack body against the pivot stop on the lifting arm. By doing this the jack will be vertical when the vehicle is raised. Turn the jack handle clockwise to raise the car just sufficiently to enable the wheel to be changed.

Having raised the jack, check that it's secure and the wheel chocks are still in position, then take off the wheel nuts and wheel.

Fit the spare wheel, and finger tighten the nuts (ensuring that their rounded ends face the wheel) then lower and remove the jack. The wheel nuts must now be fully tightened. Don't bend the spanner doing this — just make sure they're firmly tight, but remember they'll have to come off again sometime! (It's not absolutely necessary, but advisable, to recheck the nuts for tightness, later after some miles have been covered). Finally, refit the hub plate and remove chocks.

On models fitted with Rostyle wheels, the centre medallion can be transferred to the newly fitted wheel by unclipping it from the changed wheel and springing it into the replacement wheel central orifice.

Don't forget to check the pressure in the spare tyre before driving off. If you haven't got a tyre pressure gauge, or if you haven't checked the spare for months and it looks a bit soft, drive carefully to the nearest garage and check the pressure there. Don't forget to have the punctured tyre mended, either!

Maintenance of lights

Failure of any of the car's external lights can not only lay you open to prosecution if you're driving, but also constitutes a safety hazard. It's for this reason that we recommend carrying a spare set of the main bulbs, and their replacement has been included in this Chapter as we think a lamp failure should be regarded as an emergency. For your own safety as well as everyone else's, don't let your Cavalier join the large number of vehicles, that can be seen driving around any night after dark with one or more of the obligatory lights not working. Here's how to prevent it.

Headlight/sidelight bulb renewal

Open the bonnet and remove the large plastic cap from the rear of the headlight unit by screwing it anti-clockwise. Withdraw the electrical plug connector by pulling it free.

Remove the bulb retaining plate by pressing it inwards and turning it anti-clockwise. Use a piece of soft clean rag to grip the bulb to remove it. This is especially important with quartz halogen bulbs which must not be handled, but if it is accidentally touched, wipe it clean with a rag moistened with alcohol or methylated spirits before refitting it.

The sidelight bulb is incorporated into the headlight unit and can be removed by pressing it and twisting to withdraw.

Refit the bulbs using the reverse procedure to removal. Note that the metal rim on the headlight bulb has a projection which must engage on the reflector.

21

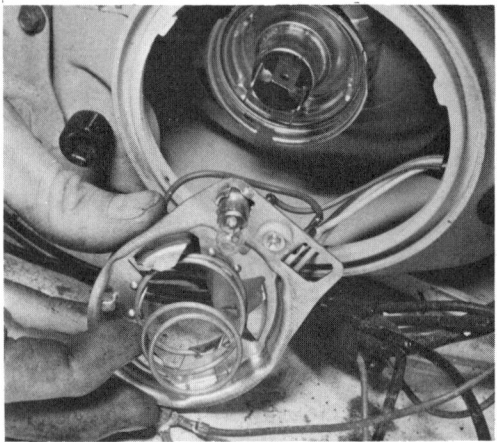

Headlight bulb retaining plate, note sidelight bulb

Withdrawing headlight bulb

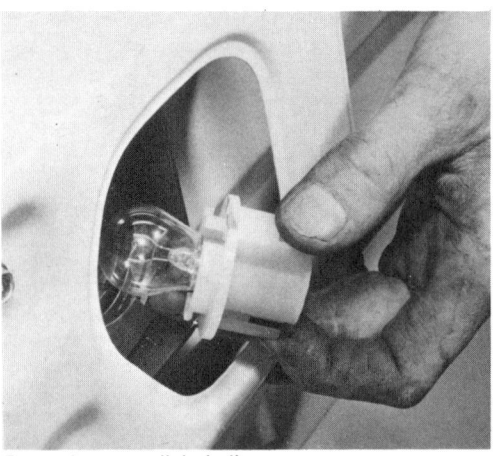

Removing a rear light bulb

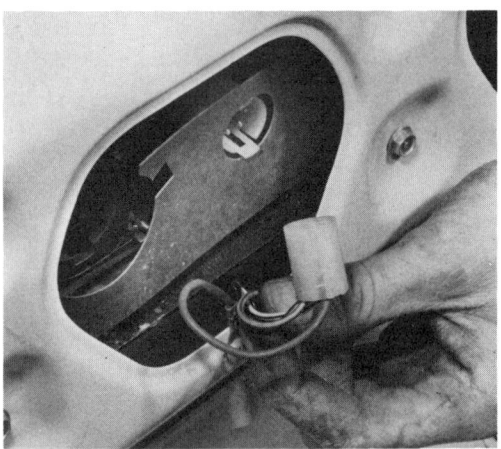

Removing the electrical plug from the rear light cluster

Interior light assembly removed

Location of fuse panel

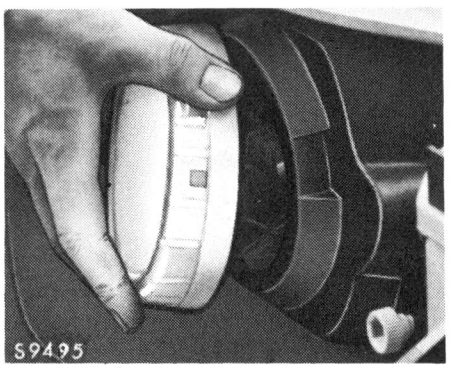

Remove the plastic cap from the rear of the headlight unit

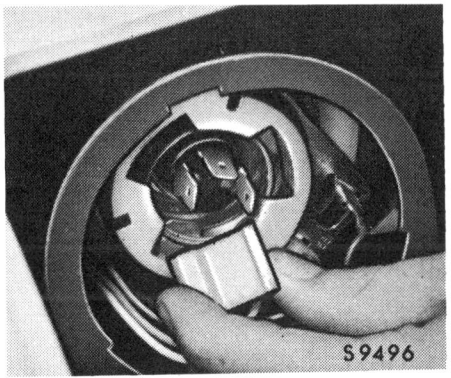

Withdraw the plug connector

The headlight alignment adjusters (arrowed)

Front indicators – renewal

On cars equipped with turn signal lights located below the front bumper, remove the two lens securing screws and withdraw the lens. The bulb can now be withdrawn.

On some models the indicator light is plugged into the headlight shell. To remove it, raise the bonnet and simply pull the light unit from the aperture.

To refit the bulb, reverse the removal procedure but test before refitting the lens.

Rear light cluster – bulb renewal

Access to the rear light cluster bulbs is gained from inside the luggage compartment. On saloon models, remove the bulbholders by turning them anti-clockwise. On Coupe models, the bulbholder is removed by pressing in the two plastic clips on the bulbholder and pulling it out.

Refitting is the reversal of the removal procedure, but note the offset pins on the stop/tail light bulb, to ensure correct refitting.

Interior and luggage compartment lights – renewal

To remove the interior light lens, carefully ease it out of the roof aperture using a thin-bladed screwdriver. The festoon-type bulb can then be renewed, or, if necessary, the wires disconnected and the lens assembly removed.

The luggage compartment light is removed in a similar manner to the interior light.

Refitting is the reverse procedure to removal.

Rear number plate light

This light is behind the rear bumper. Unscrew the two lens retaining screws and remove the lens. The bulb is housed in a plastic holder secured by a clip. Pull the holder from the clip and remove the bulb from its holder.

Refit in the reverse sequence, but don't overtighten the lens retaining screws or the lens may crack.

Fuses

Fuse failure may be diagnosed by the simultaneous failure of several electrical systems. The blown fuse may be identified by the electrical systems which are inoperative. For information on the fuse numbers and the services they protect, refer to *Vital Statistics*.

The fuses are located behind a removable panel below the instrument panel on the right of the steering column. If a fuse blows it must be replaced with a fuse of the same amps rating. If the new fuse immediately blows when the particular electrical **23** service is operated there is a fault in the system and the circuit must be carefully inspected to find the cause of the trouble.

Headlight beam adjustment

The actual setting of the headlight beam alignment is a relatively easy task, but accurate alignment can only be achieved using specialised optical equipment as installed in most garages. It is most important that the headlights are correctly set to avoid dazzling oncoming drivers and of course to comply with the regulations.

A temporary adjustment can be made by turning the two nylon screws which are located on the headlight retaining frame. These screws are accessible from inside the engine compartment. When adjusting, consideration should be given to the vehicle loading and of course it is assumed that the tyre pressures are correct. An allowance should also be made if the vehicle is used for towing.

Towing

If you are unlucky enough to have a serious breakdown and the car has to be towed home or to a garage, the following precautions should be noted:

(a) *Use a tow rope that is strong enough and long enough for the job — but not too long!*

(b) *Turn the ignition key to position 0, or I if indicators and brake lights are to be used.* **Do not** *leave the key in position B (locked)*

(c) *On models fitted with automatic transmission, move the selector lever to N. Towing speed must not exceed 30 mph (48 kph) and the maximum permissible distance is 30 miles (48 km)*

(d) *If the automatic transmission is faulty or suspected of being so, or if the maximum permissible distance or speed will be exceeded, the propeller shaft must be disconnected. Before towing ensure that the fluid level is up to the mark and top-up if necessary*

Save It!

Economy should, with today's ever-increasing prices, be foremost in the mind for the average car owner. After the initial expenditure on buying your Cavalier, your outlays have really only just begun. The car needs to be taxed and insured before you can take it on the road. Taking it, and indeed keeping it on the road requires fuel in the tank, lubrication, maintenance and repairs, all of which can rapidly consume your hard-earned cash.

Running a car is bound to cost money, but in many cases savings can be made. Obviously your road fund licence is something that will have to be paid for with no possibility of any saving. But things like fuel, oil, tyres, spare parts, accessories and even the price of your insurance can cost you less if you're prepared to shop around.

Even the price required for a certain repair can vary as much as 30% from garage to garage, so the moral must be to look at all the possibilities and prices before finally committing yourself.

Tyres

As you may know, Cavaliers are fitted with radial-ply tyres as standard equipment. Although radial tyres aren't cheap, they're definitely superior to the cross-ply tyre in both roadholding and wear potential. Don't be tempted to fit cross-ply tyres to your Cavalier as a means of saving a few pounds — the handling of the car will probably be very poor if you do fit them. When purchasing tyres, try to shop around, you've probably got a few tyre specialists in your area who give good discounts and free fitting service; and remember that your local garage or Vauxhall dealer may be the most expensive place to buy new tyres.

Obviously it's best to purchase one of the well known brands of tyre, but in recent years quite a few names have appeared on the scene, some of which can offer favourable price reductions. If you're considering buying tyres of a lesser known brand name, try to first acquire some independent information as to their safety and reliability.

Many suppliers give fair discounts on their tyres; some, on presentation of membership cards of certain clubs and organisations, will reduce their price even more.

In any event, tyres are expensive, and mention of their care must be made. Under-inflated tyres will cause excessive drag which will, in the short term, cause extra fuel to be consumed and if not quickly rectified will greatly accelerate their wear. Over-inflated tyres, whilst not causing so much drag, can

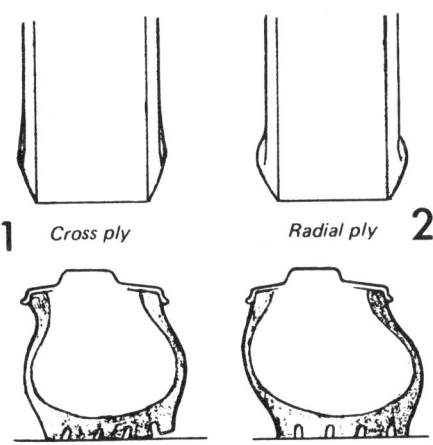

Cross ply and radial ply tyres. The difference in the construction of the two types of tyre gives them very different characteristics. The cross ply (1) has a uniformly strong tread and wall bracing. This gives it better cushioning properties but allows some deformation on bad surfaces and cambers. The radial ply tyre (2) has a supple wall and a firmly braced tread, ensuring that the maximum area of tread is kept in contact with the road despite suspension angle changes and road camber effects. On no account should the two types of tyre be mixed on the same axle

be dangerous and will wear to an abnormal tread pattern very quickly.

It's a good practice to inspect your tyres on a regular basis. Check the sidewalls, both inboard and outboard of the tyre for any cuts or damaged areas. Have a good look at the tread pattern and its depth; remember that a pattern that's not 1 mm deep for 75% of its area is illegal. We hope that you won't allow your tyres to wear to this extent, because not only is it illegal, it's also extremely dangerous and has been the cause of many serious accidents.

Batteries

Next to tyres, batteries are the most commonly found parts sold by specialists. A top quality battery may cost up to three times the price of the cheapest one that'll fit your car.

Once again, price is related to the quality of the product, but isn't necessarily directly proportional. A battery with a twelve month guarantee ought to last that long and a little bit more, but batteries always seem to fail at embarrassing or inconvenient times so it's worthwhile getting something a little bit better. Many of the accessory shops and tyre dealers sell good quality batteries with two or three year guarantees. Buy one of these – it'll be worthwhile in the long run and still cost quite a bit less than the dearest ones around. And if you look after it, it'll look after you, too.

Exhaust systems

The average car gets through several exhaust systems in the course of its life, the actual number depending on the sort of journeys for which the car's used (lots of short journeys will mean condensation remaining inside the exhaust system and helping it to rust out more quickly).

The best place to go when your car needs a new exhaust (or maybe just part of the system) is one of the specialist 'exhaust centres' which have sprung up in recent years. They keep huge stocks to fit most mass-produced cars, and offer free fitting as well as discount prices on the parts themselves. You'll almost certainly show a worthwhile saving compared with getting your Vauxhall dealer to fit the exhaust (which will involve labour charges as well).

If you're planning to keep your car for several years it would certainly be worth thinking about an exhaust system made from stainless steel. It'll normally cost you considerably more than an ordinary mild steel replacement, but on the other hand should last the remainder of the car's life. If you're interested, talk it over with one of the exhaust specialists – they're usually stockists of the stainless steel kind too.

Lubricants and the like

Good cheap engine oils are available, but because it's so difficult to find out which cheap ones *are* good, it's safest to stay clear of them. There are plenty of good multigrade engine oils on the market and quite a few are available at sensible prices from the DIY motoring and accessory shops.

Unless circumstances should force you to, don't buy oil in pint or half-litre cans. This is the most expensive way of buying, particularly if it's from a filling station. The big 5-litre (they used to be one gallon) cans are adequate for most purposes, and contain just about the right amount for an engine oil change; an extra can for topping-up between oil changes will probably be required, particularly if your pride and joy happens to be a bit of an oil burner.

Oil is also available in larger drums (which can be fitted with a tap) sometimes at an even bigger price saving. A telephone call or visit to nearby wholesalers may well prove worthwhile.

Antifreeze is always cheaper if you go to the motoring shops, but bulk buying doesn't normally apply because you never need to buy it in any real quantity.

As for greases, brake fluid, etc, you'll save a little at the motoring shops but again you'll never need large quantities – just make sure you buy something that's good quality.

Fuel

Your car's designed to run on a particular grade of fuel (star rating). Don't buy fuel that's of a higher rating than this, because you're wasting your money. On the other hand, if you buy a lower rating fuel your engine performance (and probably your engine too) will suffer. If you are forced to buy inferior fuel, drive carefully until you can get the correct grade; in these circumstances it's also beneficial to retard the ignition by a couple of degrees, but you've got the bother of resetting it again later.

Additives

Oil and fuel additives have been with us for a long time and no doubt will be around for many years to come. It's pretty unlikely that there are any bad additives around, but there's not a great deal of evidence to suggest that there are many good ones. The major oil maufacturers will tell you that their oils are adequate on their own, in which case you'll only need additives if the oil you're using isn't much good. A fuel additive of the upper cylinder lubricant type is generally accepted as a good thing, one of its main functions being to prevent carbon building up around the piston rings and ring grooves, which means that the piston rings can seal more effectively.

Smiths 'Milemiser', a useful aid to economical driving

Economy devices

If we could believe everything published about economy devices, we'd be able to fit the lot and end up with a car that would save more fuel than it used! Obviously this isn't going to happen, and the evidence produced by the motoring magazines doesn't lend much weight to the various manufacturers' arguments. If you're considering fitting any of these items (which range from manifold modifiers to spark boosters and fuel pressure regulators), try to get hold of some independent reports before parting with your money.

Vacuum gauge

Also known as a performance gauge or fuel consumption gauge, this can loosely be termed an economy device because its purpose is to tell you how to use performance in the most efficient way. An engine that's running efficiently will be using all the fuel/air mixture in the inlet manifold for any given throttle opening, and in doing so causes a fairly high suction past the throttle butterfly. The maximum suction it can produce varies, but could be over 20 inches of mercury (that's around 10 lbf/in²) relative to atmospheric pressure. If you've got one of these gauges, (and there's some information about fitting one in *The Personal Touch*) try to drive with the maximum vacuum reading all the time and you'll certainly save some money on fuel.

Engine tuning

Depending on which way you use the term, engine tuning may mean more, or less, return for your money. If an engine's tuned in order to obtain more speed (which will probably mean fitting additional or modified engine components), you'll obviously gain in the performance department but lose out economically.

Tuning for economy really means maintaining your engine in its original form as specified and prepared by the manufacturer. You may be able to get different jets for the carburettor to give a better fuel return, but any saving here will be sure to reduce the overall performance of the vehicle.

The best and most important factor in keeping your engine in a good state of tune is regular maintenance. Look after the spark plugs, distributor points, ignition timing, carburettor adjustments, air cleaners and valve clearances and you should get the best returns for your money. With all these things in order, your car's performance will be as efficient as it was meant to be, the rest is up to you as the driver.

Driving habits

Assuming that your car's in a decent state of tune, there's still a lot you can do towards improving its economy by the way you drive it.

How often have you been tempted to do a racing start from the traffic lights, or see how fast a journey can be completed, for no particular reason? Impatient 'blipping' of the throttle whilst waiting in traffic queues, allowing the clutch to engage with a juddering sound, harsh braking and cornering, all these habits are really quite unnecessary and you'll pay dearly for them in fuel and spare parts.

Use the pedals as softly as possible. When pressing the accelerator, only do so as far as required, the clutch should be engaged with the price of a replacement in mind; allow time for the engine to slow you down when approaching corners, junctions, or queues, rather than applying the brakes at the last moment; use the gears with a little more respect. You'd be surprised to learn that your journeys aren't taking that much longer and your visits to the filling station will surely cost you less.

Roof racks

A roof rack can be the answer to your holiday luggage problems, or to carrying an awkward object, but you're not likely to need it all the year round. Wind resistance on a loaded rack can increase your fuel consumption by as much as 30%, and an empty rack can increase it by around 10%. So the moral must surely be – don't use a roof rack unless you really have to, and always remove it when it's not in use.

Insurance

Like some of the other things we've discussed, the service you're going to get from your insurance company will be related to the cost of the cover obtained. A cheap policy's good until you need to make a claim, and then the sort of snags you're going **27**

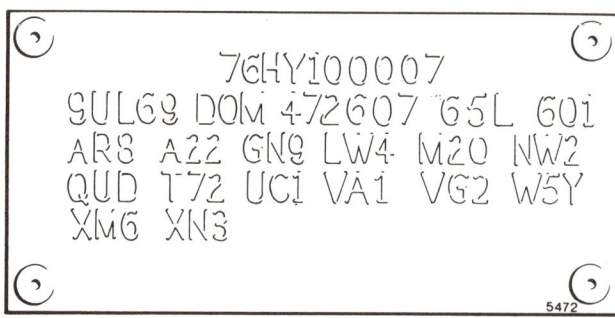

The vehicle identification plates

The engine number location on the 1256 cc engine

The engine number on a 1584 cc engine

to come across are 'How do I get hold of an assessor to inspect the damage?' or 'How will it affect my No Claims Bonus?'

There are one or two legitimate ways of reducing the policy premium, perhaps by insuring for 'owner driver only', or 'two named drivers', or an agreement to pay the first £20 or so of any claim. Many large companies have a discount scheme for their employees if they use the same insurance company; this also applies to bank and Civil Service employees. You may also get a better bargain by insuring through one of the Motoring Associations if you're a member.

What it all adds up to is: (1) Insure well: (2) See what you can get in the way of discounts; and (3) Find out exactly what you're covered for.

Buying spare parts

Sooner or later the time will almost certainly come when you need a few items other than oils and grease. If you're buying on an exchange basis (eg brake shoes) please do remember to clean up the parts that you're going to exchange. Wherever possible, take along the old component for a comparison. Spare parts and accessories are available from many sources, but the following should serve as a good guide when they're required.

Officially appointed Vauxhall dealers: Although a Vauxhall garage should be able to supply just about everything for your car, it will generally be found that the prices are higher than you need pay.

Other garages: In recent years the big British car manufacturers have introduced a replacement parts scheme whereby they market parts for each other's cars under trade names such as Mopar, Unipart and Motorcraft. You'll pay the same prices as you would from the Vauxhall dealer, but you may well find that your local Leyland or Ford dealer can supply you with guaranteed parts for your Vauxhall, and this can be a great convenience.

Accessory shops: These are usually the best places for getting your distributor contact breaker points, oil filters, brake shoes, spark plugs, fan belts, lubricants, touch-up paint etc – the very things you're going to need for the general servicing of the car. They also sell general accessories and charge lower prices, but, what's equally important, they have convenient opening hours and can often be found not far from home.

Motor factors: Good factors will stock all the more important components of the engine, gearbox, suspension and braking systems, and often provide guaranteed parts on an exchange basis. They're particularly useful to the more advanced do-it-yourself motorist.

Vehicle identification numbers

When ordering spare parts (and sometimes accessories), the very least you must know is the model and year of manufacture of your car. For some items this is all you need to know, but there will soon come a time when you're asked for the engine number or vehicle identification number (which you'd always meant to make a note of but just hadn't got round to it!).

The vehicle identification number plate is located inside the engine compartment on top of the front end panel. The plate is marked with the vehicle chassis and designation number and the colour code. Also shown is the maximum gross weight for the car.

The engine number on 1256 cc engines is stamped on a pad on the right-hand side of the engine, to the rear of the front end of the exhaust manifold. On larger engines, the number is to be found stamped on a pad on the left-hand side of the cylinder block. The prefixes 165, 195 or 205 denote engine capacity.

Make a note of these numbers now, in your diary or in the back of this book.

Vital Statistics

The following pages contain the more important technical specifications of the Cavalier range. We're not suggesting that you need to know all these facts and figures, but you'll find it necessary to refer to this Section for the various adjustments and settings you need during the routine servicing work.

We'll start with the engine details and work our way through this car ...

ENGINE

Type   4-cylinder, in-line, ohv (1256 cc) or ohc (larger engines), water-cooled

Cubic capacity
1300 models   1256 cc (76.6 cu in)
1600 models   1584 cc (92.0 cu in)
1900 models   1897 cc (115.8 cu in)
2000 models   1979 cc (120.8 cu in)

Bore and stroke	*Bore*	*Stroke*
1300 models	3.18 in (80.98 mm)	2.40 in (60.96 mm)
1600 models	3.35 in (85.0 mm)	2.75 in (69.8 mm)
1900 models	3.66 in (93.0 mm)	2.75 in (69.8 mm)
2000 models	3.73 in (95.0 mm)	2.75 in (69.8 mm)

Compression ratio
1300 models   8.7:1
1600 models   8.8:1
1900 models   8.8:1
2000 models   9.0:1

Firing order
All models   1,3,4,2

Valve clearances
1300 models (engine hot)   0.008 in (0.20 mm) inlet and exhaust
1600 and 1900 models (engine hot)   0.012 in (0.30 mm) inlet and exhaust
2000 models   Preset (hydraulic tappets)

Maximum power output (DIN)
1300 models   57 bhp @ 5600 rpm

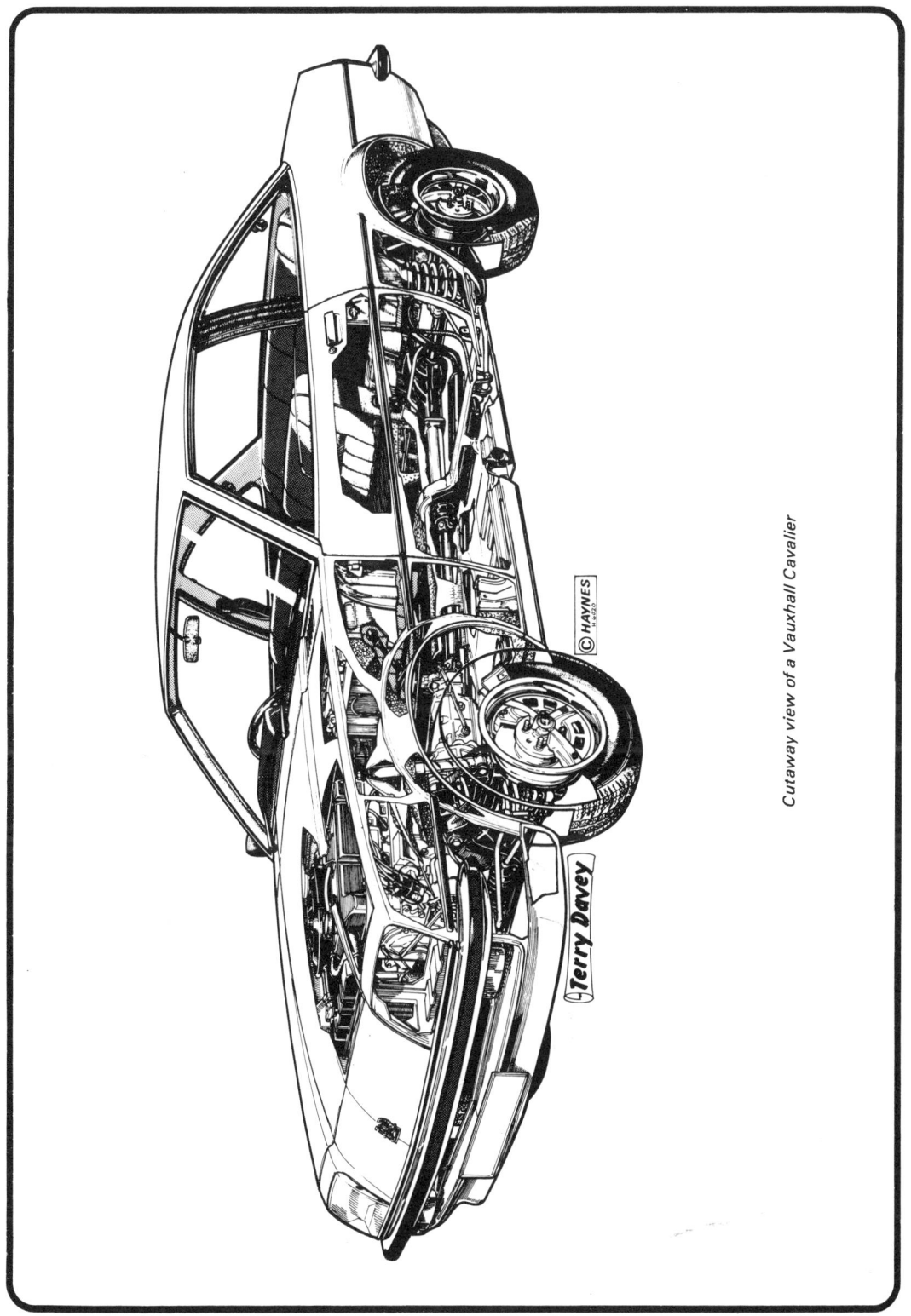

Cutaway view of a Vauxhall Cavalier

HAYNES

Terry Davey

1600 models	75 bhp @ 5000 rpm
1900 models	90 bhp @ 4800 rpm
2000 models	100 bhp @ 5400 rpm

Lubrication system

Oil pump (all models)	Gear type, driven by helical gears
Nominal pressure (all models)	At least 30 lbf/in² (2.0 kgf/cm²) at 30 mph
Oil filter:	
1300 models	Full flow, renewable element type
All other models	Full flow, disposable cartridge type
Oil type (all models, normal use)	20W-50 multigrade
Sump capacity (including filter):	
1300 models	5.0 Imp pints (2.84 litres)
All other models	6.7 Imp pints (3.80 litres)

COOLING SYSTEM

System type	Pressurised, thermo-syphon, pump-assisted and fan cooled

Thermostat

Type (all models)	Wax pellet
Opening temperature (all models)	189°F (87°C)

Radiator cap release pressure

All models	13.2 to 15.2 lbf/in² (0.42 to 1.06 kgf/cm²)

Fanbelt tension

Al models	0.25 in (6 mm) deflection under firm thumb pressure midway between water pump and alternator

Antifreeze type

All models	Ethylene glycol, BS 3151 or 3152

FUEL SYSTEM

Air cleaner

All models	Renewable paper element type

Fuel pump

1300 models	Mechanical, driven from camshaft, with mesh type filter
All other models	Mechanical, driven from distributor shaft, with mesh type filter

Carburettor type

1300 models	Stromberg 150CD-SEU
1600 and 1900 models	Solex 35 PDSI, or Solex 32/32 DIDTA, or Zenith 35/40 INAT
2000 models	GM Varajet II

Idling speed

All models	800 to 850 rpm

Fuel tank capacity

1300 models	8 Imp gallons (36.4 litres)
All other models	11 Imp gallons (50.0 litres)

IGNITION SYSTEM

Spark plugs
Type:

1300 models	AC 42XLS or equivalent
All other models	AC 42FS or equivalent

Gap:

1300 models	0.040 in (1.0 mm)
All other models	0.030 in (0.75 mm)

Contact breaker points gap
All models   0.020 in (0.50 mm)

Ignition timing (static)

1300 models	9° BTDC
All other models	5° BTDC

CLUTCH

Type   Single dry plate, diaphragm spring, cable operated

Clutch pedal free travel
All models   Nil

Clutch fork setting dimension

1300 models	Not applicable
All other models	4.29 in (109 mm)

MANUAL TRANSMISSION

Type   4 forward speeds and one reverse. Synchromesh on all forward speeds

Ratios	*1300*	*1600 and 1900*	*2000*
First	3.460	3.428	3.640
Second	2.213	2.156	2.120
Third	1.404	1.366	1.340
Fourth	1.000	1.000	1.000
Reverse	3.317	3.317	3.317

Oil capacity   1.1 Imp pints (0.56 litres)
All other models   1.9 Imp pints (1.10 litres)

Oil type   SAE 90EP gear oil

AUTOMATIC TRANSMISSION

Type   GM type OH or OG, 3 forward speeds and 1 reverse

Mechanical ratios (typical)

First	2.40
Second	1.48

33

VITAL STATISTICS

Third	1.00
Reverse	1.92

Lubricant capacity
Refill (all models) — 4.4 Imp pints (2.5 litres)

Lubricant type
All models — Dexron automatic transmission fluid

FINAL DRIVE

Axle type
All models — Semi-floating, hypoid

Axle ratios

1300 models	4.11
1600 models	3.70
1900 models	3.67
2000 models	3.44

BRAKING SYSTEM

System type — Discs front, drums rear. Dual hydraulic circuit with servo assistance. Handbrake mechanical to rear wheels

Brake pedal free travel — 0.24 to 0.31 in (6 to 8 mm)

Disc pad minimum thickness — 0.08 in (2 mm)

Brake fluid type — SAE J1703

ELECTRICAL SYSTEM

Type — 12V, negative earth, alternator with integral regulator and battery

Battery capacity

1300 models	36 amp hours
All other models	44 amp hours

Alternator

Make	Bosch or Delco-Remy
Output	45 amps maximum
Brush length:	
Bosch	0.2 in (5 mm) minimum protrusion
Delco-Remy	0.4 in (10 mm) minimum length

Starter motor

Make	Bosch or Delco-Remy
Brush length:	
Bosch	0.51 in (13 mm) minimum
Delco-Remy	0.38 in (9.5 mm) minimum

Fuses

Fuse No	Rating	Circuit protected
1	5 amp	Right-hand side and tail lamps
2	5 amp	Left-hand side and tail lamps, number plate lamp, instrument and control lamps. Where applicable, fog rear guard lamps
3	8 amp	Interior lamp, headlamp flasher, hazard warning system Where applicable, luggage boot lamp, radio and clock
4	8 amp	Windscreen wipers and washer. Where applicable, automatic choke
5	8 amp	Heater motor, reversing lamp. On automatic transmission models, starter inhibitor switch
6	8 amp	Stoplamps and turn signal lamps
7	16 amp	Rear window demister
8	8 amp	Horn. Where applicable, cigar lighter and fog lamp switch
9	8 or 16 amp	Spare
10	8 or 16 amp	Where applicable, fog lamp relay; otherwise spare

SUSPENSION AND STEERING

Front suspension

Type — Upper and lower wishbones, coil springs, telescopic shock absorbers, anti-roll bar

Hub bearing endfloat — 0.001 to 0.004 in (0.02 to 0.10 mm)

Rear suspension

Type — Trailing arm, coil springs, Panhard rod and anti-roll bar. Telescopic shock absorbers

Steering

Type — Rack and pinion with collapsible column and flexible coupling

Turning circle — 30.2 ft (9.2 m)

Camber — 0°20 positive to 5° 30 negative

Toe-in — 0.11 to 0.19 in (2.8 to 4.8 mm)

GENERAL DIMENSIONS

Wheelbase — 99.1 in (2.518 m)

Track (front and rear) — 54.1 in (1.375 m)

Overall length

Saloon — 175 in (4.445 m)

Coupe — 177 in (4.496 m)

Overall width

L models — 65.1 in (1.654 m)

GL models — 65.4 in (1.662 m)

Coupe — 64.7 in (1.650 m)

Overall height

Saloon — 54.3 in (1.380 m)

Coupe — 52.4 in (1.330 m)

VITAL STATISTICS

Kerb weights

1300 L models:	
2-door	1973 lb (895 kg)
4-door	2017 lb (915 kg)
1600 L models:	
2-door	2161 lb (980 kg)
4-door	2205 lb (1000 kg)
1600 GL models	2205 lb (1000 kg)
2000 GL models	2205 lb (1000 kg)
2000 GLS models	2205 lb (1000 kg)

With automatic transmission add 44 lb (20 kg)

Tools for the Job

For anyone intending to tackle car servicing, a selection of good down-to-earth tools is a basic requirement. The initial outlay, even though it may appear to be something approaching the national defence budget, could well be less than the labour charges for one full service; on top of this, you should be paying less for the oil and any new parts by getting them yourself so provided you've two or three hours to spare, you must be on to a winner.

A small but important point when buying tools is the quality. You don't have to buy the very best in the shop but, on the other hand, the cheapest probably aren't much good. Have a word with the manager or proprietor if you're in doubt. He'll tell you what's good value for money.

It's very difficult to tell you exactly what you're going to need, but the list below should be a great help in building up a good tool kit. Combination spanners (ring one end, open-ended the other) are recommended because, although more expensive than double open-ended ones, they give the advantages of both types.

Combination spanners – 10, 11, 13, 14 and 17 mm
Gearbox/rear axle drain plug key
Adjustable spanner – 9 inch

Spark plug spanner (with rubber insert)
2 BA box spanner
Spark plug gap adjustment tool
Set of feeler gauges
Oil filter strap wrench (not 1300 models)
Screwdriver – 4 in blade x $\frac{1}{4}$ in dia (plain)
Screwdriver – 4 in blade x $\frac{1}{4}$ in dia (crosshead)
Pliers – 6 inch
Junior hacksaw
Tyre pump
Tyre pressure gauge
Grease gun
Oil can
Fine emery cloth or oilstone
Wire brush (small)
Funnel (medium size)
Hydraulic jack or strong scissor type

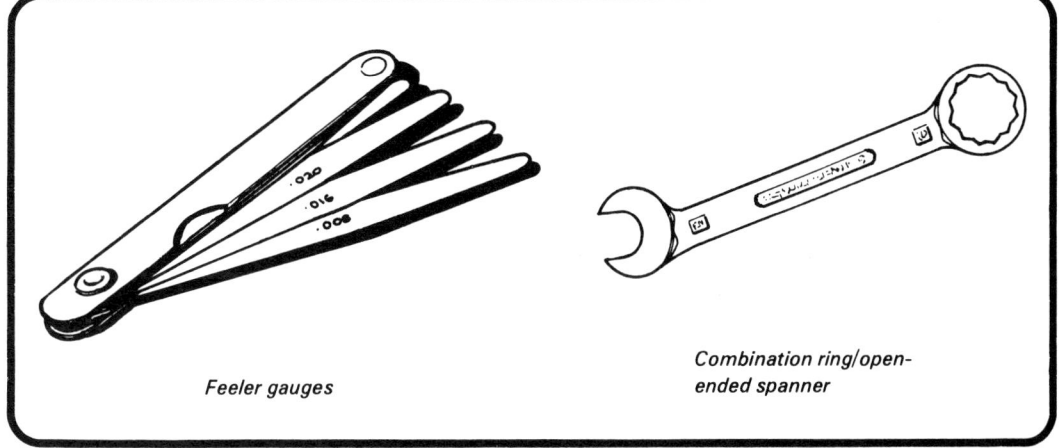

Feeler gauges

Combination ring/open-ended spanner

Pair of axle stands (concrete or wooden blocks will do if you're careful about choosing them)
Hose brush

You may find that a pair of metal ramps is a very useful investment, providing an alternative to the jack or axle stands when you want to get at the underside of the car but don't need to remove the wheel(s). Most ramps available give a lift of between 9 inches and 1ft and you can, of course, drive either the front or back end of the car on to them – but you'll still need to engage a gear and chock the other two wheels for safety's sake.

When it comes to oil changing, you can improvise a suitable container in which to catch the waste oil by slitting open one side of an old 5-litre can – but you've got the problem of handling and disposing of it afterwards. A useful product which helps overcome both these snags is the Drainer Can, seen in use in the photograph.

Made of special plastic to withstand hot engine oil, it has a capacity of about 8 litres (14 pints) and permits the old oil to be stored or transported in a horizontal or vertical position, for disposal at your local garage or in some other acceptable way. For convenience, the can has a carrying handle and pouring nozzle, and it's 100% leakproof even when full, as we can testify.

Hopefully, your attempts at car servicing are going to show you that it can all be worthwhile, and having worked your way through the various jobs listed in the Service Schedules you'll be able to see that there are many others which can be done without becoming a mechanical wizard. For this purpose, Haynes publish two first-class Owner's Workshop Manuals for the Cavaliers – one for 1300 models, the other for the larger-engined models – which detail just about every operation that can conceivably be done on these cars. It'll mean buying a few more tools, but to hell with it – you're out to save yourself some money and get a good job done in the process.

While we're talking of tools, it's worth mentioning some of the tune-up aids that are on the market. A visit to a good motor accessory shop can be an enlightening experience, just to show you the sort of things available. Later in this book, you'll find a bit about 'bolt-on goodies', but all we'll concern ourselves with here are the items below.

Stroboscopic timing light

The most accurate way of checking ignition timing (that's the time at which the spark occurs) is with the engine running, and for this stroboscopic (strobe) light is used. This is connected to a spark plug lead and the beam is shone on to the crankshaft pulley marks. Any proprietary light is supplied with

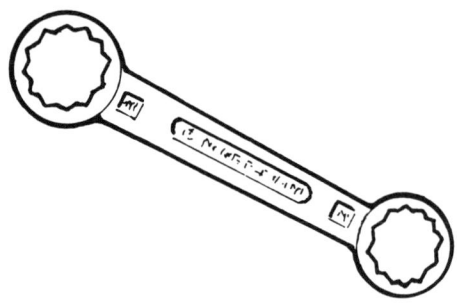

Double ended ring spanner

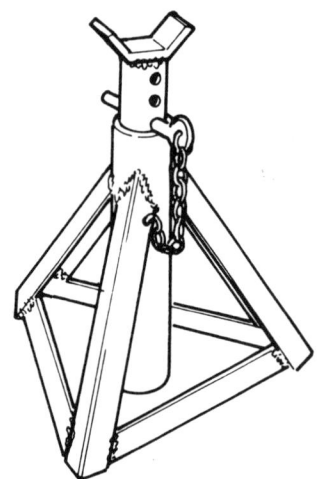

Axle stand

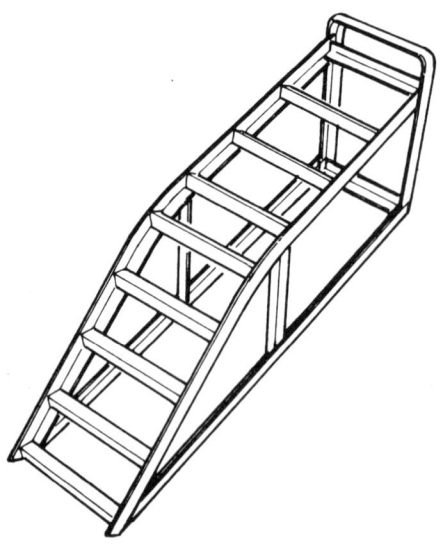

Steel ramp

A Drainer Can in use during an oil change

full connecting and operating instructions.

Dwell angle meter

This is used for measuring the period of time for which the distributor points remain closed during the ignition cycle of one cylinder, and provides a more accurate method of setting-up the ignition than can be done by simply setting the points gap. Dwell angle meters normally incorporate a tachometer (rev counter if you prefer), which can be useful for checking engine idle speed.

Cylinder compression gauge

This is very useful for tracing the cause of a fall-off in engine performance. It consists of a pressure gauge and non-return valve, and is simply screwed into a spark plug hole while the engine is turned over on the starter.

Two other useful items are a hydrometer, which is used for checking the specific gravity of the battery electrolyte (this will tell you if you have a dud cell which won't hold a charge), and a 12-volt lamp on an extension lead with crocodile clips which can be connected to the battery terminals.

Care of your tools

Having bought a reasonable set of tools and equipment, it's the easiest thing in the world to abuse them. After use, always wipe off any dirt and grease using a clean, dry cloth before putting them away. Never leave them lying around after they've been used. A simple rack on the garage wall, for things you don't need to carry in the car, is a good idea.

Keep all your spanners and the like in a metal box – you can wrap some rags around them to stop them rattling if you're going to carry them in the boot. Any gauges and meters should be carefully put away so that they don't get damaged or rusty. Do take a little care over maintaining your tools too. Screwdriver blades, for example, inevitably lose their keen edges, and a little timely attention with a file won't go amiss. **39**

Service Scene

We've now discussed some of the more important features of your car and also given some thoughts to equally important things like tools, money saving and so on. Now to the nitty-gritty of servicing – perhaps the very thing you've dreaded for so long? It's not as mysterious or as difficult as you think ...

A trend has grown up with modern cars to reduce the amount of servicing required, which tends to make people think the car will go on forever without any regular attention because half the bits aren't there any more! It's still important to carry out all the servicing and inspections at regular intervals to keep the car safe, to prolong its active life, and to maintain a sensible resale value.

The old maxim of 'prevention is better than cure' could never be more aptly applied than in connection with car servicing. Whether it be casting your eagle eye over the general workings of the car or getting down to the service tasks in a workmanlike (or workwomanlike) fashion, it's all going to be worthwhile in the long run. Remember that a worn part won't put itself right, and isn't a thing to be lived with. Fix it as soon as you find it, even if it's not time for the next service.

In this Chapter, we've tried to present the servicing tasks in a logical way to minimize the amount of jacking up, etc, which may be a prelude to the actual job. The items listed are basically those recommended by the car manufacturer, but are supplemented by some additional ones which we think are well worth the extra trouble.

If you've recently bought the car the safest thing is to go right through all the Service Schedules, unless you can really satisfy yourself that the previous owner was as meticulous about things as you'd like to be. If you don't use the car regularly, and aren't likely to clock up the mileage until well after the time interval, always use the time interval as the basis for servicing. You'll notice that there are Spring and Autumn schedules too, just so that you can make sure the car's in the best possible state for the season ahead.

Certain adverse operating conditions will affect the engine oil change intervals. If you only use your car for short journeys or consistent stop-start operation, or in extremes of cold or heat, you should reduce your oil change mileage from the normal 6000 miles to 3000 miles. Similarly, when driving regularly in very dusty conditions it will be necessary to change the air cleaner element more often, say every 6000 miles.

Safety

Accidents do happen, but 99% of them can be prevented by taking a little care. We're going to list a few points which should reduce any accident risk, and we'd like you to read through them before starting work - it could prove to be very worthwhile.

DON'T run the engine in the garage with the doors closed.

DON'T work in an inspection pit with the engine running, the fumes will tend to concentrate at the lowest point.

DO keep long hair, sleeves, ties and the like well clear of any rotating parts when the engine's running.

DON'T grab hold of ignition HT leads when the engine's running – there's just a possibility of an electric shock, particularly if the leads are dirty or wet.

DO chock the rear wheels when jacking up the front of the car, and vice versa. Where possible, also apply the handbrake and engage first or reverse gear.

DON'T rely on the car jack when you're working underneath. Axle stands, or wooden or concrete blocks should be used, but choose the points of support sensibly to prevent damaging anything.

DO wipe up grease or oil from the floor if you spill any (and you will do, sooner or later).

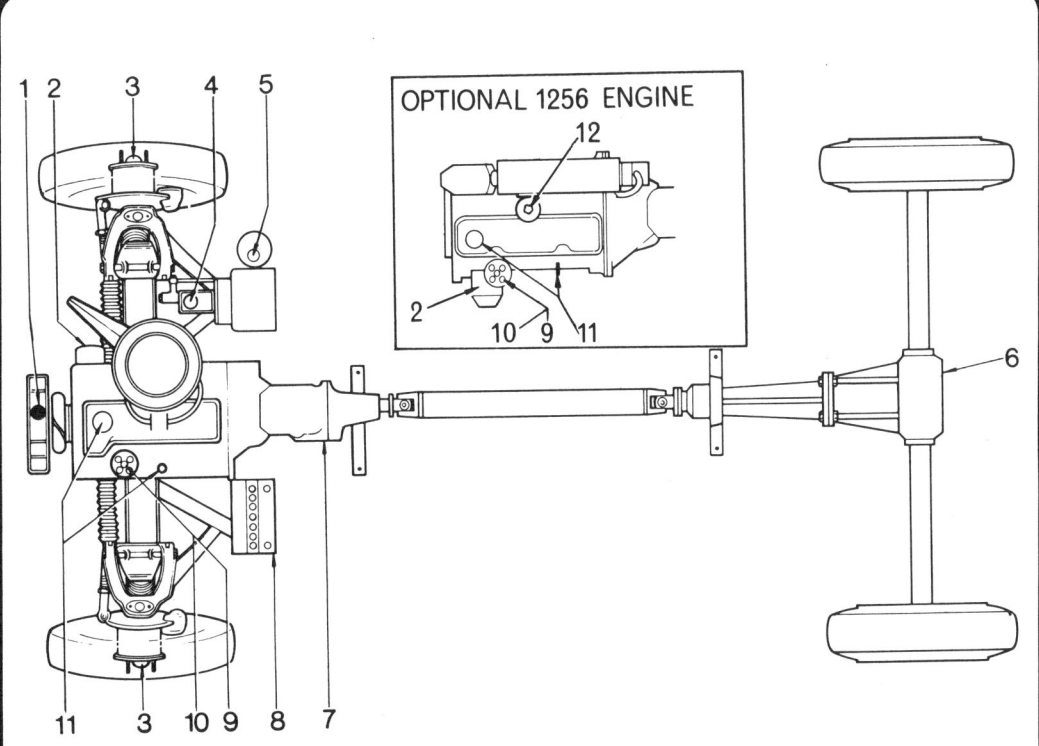

OPTIONAL 1256 ENGINE

Lubrication Chart

Component	Recommended lubricant
1 Radiator	Antifreeze to BS 3151 or 3152
2 Oil filter	–
3 Front hub bearings	Lithium based grease
4 Brake hydraulic reservoir	Hydraulic fluid to SAE J1703
5 Windscreen washer reservoir	Windscreen cleaning fluid
6 Rear axle	SAE 90EP hypoid gear oil
7 Manual gearbox	SAE 90EP hypoid gear oil
Automatic transmission	Dexron automatic transmission fluid
8 Battery	Distilled water
9 Distributor cam lobe	General purpose grease
10 Distributor felt pad	Multigrade engine oil
11 Engine	Multigrade engine oil SAE 20W/50
12 Carburettor hydraulic damper	Multigrade engine oil SAE 20W/50

DO get someone to check regularly that everything's OK if you're likely to be spending some time underneath the car.

DON'T use a file or similar tool without a handle. The tang can give you a nasty gash if something goes wrong.

DO make sure when you're using a spanner, that it's the right size for the nut and it's properly fitted before tightening or loosening.

DO brush away any drilling swarf with an old paintbrush – never with your fingers.

DON'T allow battery acid or battery terminal corrosion to contact the skin or clothes. If it should happen, wash off immediately with plenty of cold running water.

DON'T rush any job, because this is how mistakes are made. If you don't think you'll finish the job in time, do it tomorrow, but try not to make this a reason for forgetting about it.

DO take care when pouring brake fluid. If it spills on the paintwork and isn't removed immediately, it'll take the paint off. And wash your hands well afterwards as it's poisonous.

SERVICE SCHEDULES
WEEKLY, BEFORE A LONG JOURNEY OR EVERY 250 MILES (400 KM)

The following tools, lubricants, etc, are likely to be needed:

Tyre pressure gauge, lint-free cloth, engine oil, distilled water, automatic transmission fluid (if applicable).

1   Check radiator coolant level

This should preferably be done with the engine cool, but if it is quite hot and the cap has to be removed, first place a good sized cloth over the cap. This will prevent any escaping steam or boiling water from scalding your hand on releasing the cap. Turn the cap slowly in an anti-clockwise direction and at the same time press downwards on it. When the cap is partly released, allow the pressure within the system to escape before finally removing the cap.

The coolant level in the radiator should be about 1 inch (25 mm) below the bottom of the filler neck. If when topping-up you overfill it, don't worry too much as the excess will run out of the overflow pipe until the correct level is reached. Before refitting the radiator cap, ensure that the seal is in good condition and is clean.

If the cooling system contains antifreeze then the level should be topped-up using a mixture of equal strength. To continually add water only will cause the solution to be diluted and progressively lose its effective strength. If continuous topping-up is necessary then the fault should be investigated and cured before it becomes serious. The most likely cause will be a leaky hose or poor connection. The radiator or its pressure cap may also be faulty; occasionally a defective water pump will leak before it packs up, or a blown head gasket will allow water into the oilways or cylinders. When looking for leaks, antifreeze or rusty water stains sometimes give a clue as to location. It may also help to inspect the engine when it's running and fully warmed up. but beware of the fan and other moving parts, and take care not to burn or scald yourself! If the fault is not readily apparent, your Vauxhall dealer or local garage can pressure test the system and so locate any leaks.

2   Check the engine oil level

When checking the engine oil level, have the car standing on level ground. If the engine has been running, allow it to stand for a couple of minutes before checking. This will allow the oil in circulation to settle and give a true reading.

Take out the dipstick, wipe it clean and fully re-insert it. Remove it again and observe the oil level. The level should never be allowed to drop below the bottom mark on the dipstick. If the level has dropped to the lower mark, it will need approximately 2 pints (1.14 litres) for the 1256 cc engine, or 2.5 pints (1.5 litres) for the larger engined models, to top-up the level – don't overfill! If oil has to be added frequently to keep the level up you either have a bigger than average oil leak, the source of which should be obvious, or the engine is getting old and is burning a lot of oil in the cylinders.

3   Check tyre pressures

With the tyres cold, check the pressures (see Filling Station Facts). If possible use your own gauge – those or garage forecourts tend to be abused and inaccurate. Don't forget the spare wheel; the pressure here should be up to the maximum ever likely to be needed, as letting some air out is much easier than putting it in if the wheel has to be used in an emergency!

With the tyres correctly inflated, run your hands and eyes over the tyre walls and tread. This is best done with the wheel off the ground so that it can be rotated but, if you're really not feeling up to it, move the car forwards or backwards a foot or so, so that you can check all round. If you have a tyre tread depth gauge, check that the tread is at least 1 mm deep throughout at least three quarters of the tyre width.

Alternatively a 2p piece can be used as a rough guide. Insert the coin into the tread and, if it's not deeper than the distance from the row of dots to the edge of the coin, you're breaking the law, so get some replacements pretty quickly! There must be no cuts, bulges or other deformities; if these are present you

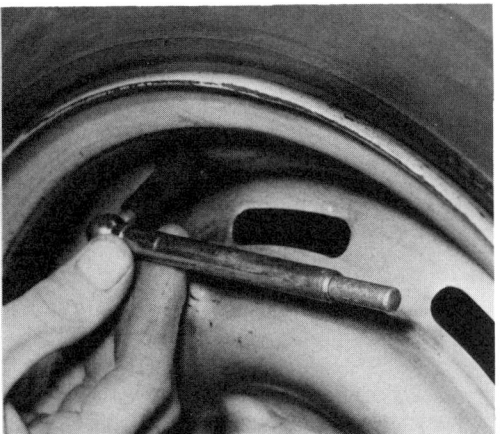

Checking tyre pressures

Check the windscreen washer reservoir level

are breaking the law again.

If you've got to buy new tyres, read the bit in *Save It!* Remember it's illegal to drive with a cross-ply and a radial-ply tyre on the same end of the car. The only permissible combination is cross-plies on the front and radials on the rear, but think of the problem you'll have if you get a puncture. For safety's sake use a complete set of tyres of the same type.

4 Check battery electrolyte level

First wipe away any dirt or moisture from the top of the battery so that none can get inside. Remove the caps or cover from the battery cells, and check the electrolyte level. Add distilled water if necessary to bring the level just above the tops of the battery plates; with the Lucas Pacemaker type, distilled water is added to the trough until all the rectangular filling slots are full and the bottom of the trough's just covered.

If for some reason you've got no distilled water you can use the frost which collects on the walls of the freezer or fridge, and allow this to melt; if you're really desperate, and as a last resort only, boil up some tap water in the kettle, allow it to cool and use that, but don't make a habit of using this or the battery will suffer in the long run.

Refit the cell caps or cover, wiping up any drops of water that were spilt, then check that the terminals are tight. A very light smear of petroleum jelly can be applied to these to help prevent any corrosion. If the weather's extremely cold, run the engine for a few minutes; this will charge the battery and mix the electrolyte which will prevent the added water from freezing.

5 Top-up windscreen washer reservoir

Add soft water as necessary to the windscreen washer reservoir, together with a little of one of the proprietary detergent products for windscreens. Add a special antifreeze sachet or methylated spirit in cold weather to prevent freezing (don't use radiator antifreeze). Finally check that the screenwasher pump and jets operate correctly.

6 Check automatic transmission fluid level (if applicable)

The automatic transmission fluid must be kept at the correct level at all times. If the transmission is overfilled the fluid will foam and cause overheating; if the level drops too low the system will malfunction and gear changes will become erratic.

Check the fluid level when the engine and transmission are at their normal operating temperatures and with the vehicle parked on level ground. Run the engine at its normal idling speed and have the selector lever in the P position (with the handbrake applied). The combined dipstick and filler cap is located at the rear of the air cleaner unit, and must be wiped clean prior to removal. Extract the dipstick and wipe it clean (use non-fluffy and clean cloth). Re-insert the stick fully, withdraw it again and observe the level which should be up to but not beyond the F mark. If the fluid has dropped to the ADD mark, about 1 pint (0.5 litre) of the recommended fluid must be added and the level rechecked.

Frequent need for topping-up indicates a fault in the system and you should have your Vauxhall dealer investigate it as soon as possible. Always use the recommended fluid and do not use oil additives of any sort.

7 Check lights, indicators and windscreen wipers

It is most important (though often overlooked) to **43**

check that your lights are in working order, and this also includes the brake lights and hazard warning system. The ignition will have to be switched on to check the brake and indicator lights. If an assistant isn't at hand, watch the reflection in a shop window or off another vehicle. To replace bulbs that aren't working see *In an Emergency*.

Check the timing of the flashes, which must be between 1 and 2 flashes a second. If too fast or slow then the flasher unit is at fault, or the earth connection to the bulb may not be good. If fitting a new flasher unit, handle it with care and ensure that the wiring connections are correct.

Check that the windscreen wipers are operating correctly (but not on a dry screen). If the blades are worn or perished change them before they start to scratch the windscreen.

EVERY 6000 MILES (10 000 KM) OR 6 MONTHS, WHICHEVER COMES FIRST

(In addition to the items listed in the Weekly/250 mile schedule)

The following tools and materials are likely to be needed:

Spark plug spanner and gap setting tool, feeler gauge, oil filter strap wrench (not for 1300 models), gearbox/back axle filler plug key, torque wrench (if available), tachometer (if available), screwdrivers and sundry spanners.

Engine oil and filter, gearbox/back axle oil, hydraulic fluid, general purpose grease, rocker cover gasket.

1 Change engine oil and filter

Note: The engine oil's normally changed at intervals of 6 months or 6000 miles, but under certain adverse conditions more frequent changing is required. Such conditions are: repeated stop/start driving where the choke is frequently being used; driving in extreme cold conditions; or driving under extremely hot conditions.

Oil changes should be made when the engine is warm, as this allows the oil to drain out more quickly. So, if it's not warm, drive around for a mile or two — this is better than leaving a cold engine idling because less wear will take place.

Now get a suitable container which will fit under the sump. It's got to be fairly shallow, and at the same time hold nearly a gallon of oil — see the remarks about the Drainer Can in *Tools for the Job*. If you're stuck, a washing up bowl is the sort of thing that will do the job, otherwise you'll end up by raising the front of the car to clear the container, which may mean that not all the oil will drain out.

Now prepare yourself for the dirty part! Lie on the ground and remove the sump drain plug. You're going to get oil on your fingers, and possibly all over your hand, so do it as quickly as possible. If by chance you drop the drain plug into the container, don't forget it's there — you're going to need it later on.

Whilst the oil is draining from the sump, turn your attention to the oil filter. There are two types of filter fitted to the Cavalier: 1300 models have a renewable element type filter, whereas all the larger engined models have a disposable cartridge type filter. Both types will still contain half a pint or so of oil, so try to be prepared for any spillage.

On 1300 models, the filter is on the left-hand side of the engine. A bolt through the centre of the filter must be unscrewed to loosen the housing. If the

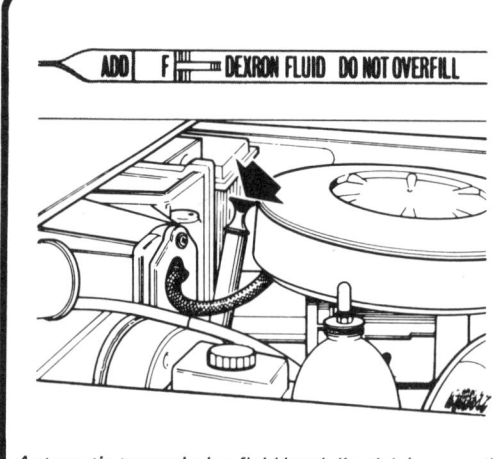

Automatic transmission fluid level dipstick (arrowed)

Cartridge type oil filter. Check the joint (arrowed) for leaks

Removing oil filter (1300 models)

Setting valve clearances (1300 models)

housing sticks in position give it a light tap to dislodge it. Hold the open end up when removing to prevent oil spillage.

Take out the old element from the housing and throw it away. Wash out the inside of the housing with paraffin and remove any sludge, then wipe dry. Note that the spring and plate around the centre bolt are a permanent fixture. Using a small screwdriver, extract the sealing ring from the circular groove in the engine block. Check that the old ring's the same size as the replacement supplied with your new filter before discarding it. Some filters are supplied with two rings, so select the one you require and insert it into the block location groove. Take care that it doesn't get distorted or damaged in any way or it'll leak. Insert the new element into its housing – either way round – and carefully place the housing and element back into position on the block, rotating the housing against the rubber sealing ring to be sure that it seats correctly. Tighten the retaining bolt securely but don't overtighten.

On 1600, 1900 and 2000 models, the filter cartridge is on the right-hand side of the engine. The cartridge is removed by unscrewing it from the retaining body. This may not be as easy as it sounds. Many filters are overtightened on assembly and are quite reluctant to be removed. In this instance ensure that the outer body is wiped completely dry and is free of oil (this should also apply to your hands!) to get a good grip. If this fails it will mean using a strap wrench, which you may be able to borrow if you don't feel like buying one. Alternatively, fit a large hose clip around the filter body; when tight this will give you extra grip and can if necessary be tapped with a hammer, but be careful what you're hitting!

On removing the old filter, wipe the joint area and check that the sealing washer is in position and not twisted. When using a new washer, smear it with some clean engine oil to ensure a good seal when the filter is fitted. Screw the new filter into position and tighten hand tight only.

All models: When the new oil filter's been fitted and the oil has finished draining from the sump, refit the drain plug – make sure that the sealing washer's in good condition – and refill with the correct grade and quantity of fresh oil. Run the engine for a minute or two, keeing a sharp eye out for leaks from the drain plug or the oil filter. If there's a leak at the filter, stop the engine, slacken the filter off and check the sealing washer. Finally stop the engine, allow a couple of minutes for the oil to drain back into the sump, re-check the level and top-up if necessary.

There's always a problem with disposing of waste oil, but if you buy it in 5-litre cans you can put the old oil in them and let the dustman take it away. The only alternative is to get some similar type of container and dispose of it in the same way. Some garages will take the old oil off your hands – they've got arrangements for disposal. Under no circumstances pour waste oil down the household drain, it's illegal as well as anti-social.

2 Adjust valve clearances

Note: *This task is unnecessary on 2000 models, which have non-adjustable hydraulic tappets.*

Although the manufacturers recommend that you check the valve clearances with the engine running, it can be a hazardous pastime for the inexperienced and we therefore suggest that you check and adjust the valves with the engine stationary. First run the engine to its normal operating temperature. It's a good idea to have a new rocker cover gasket available.

To remove the rocker cover detach the crankcase ventilation hose, the coil cover and the distributor cap **45** (see below). Loosen the bolt retaining the number three and four plug lead bracket to the inlet manifold, and then undo the rocker cover screws and carefully lift the cover clear. If the seal is broken or badly worn it must be renewed on reassembly.

The valve clearances are checked between the end of the valve stem and the rocker arm, and this gap occurs when the valve is fully closed. The engine will have to be turned over and this is best done with a suitable ring spanner fitted onto the crankshaft pulley nut – the one at the bottom driving the fanbelt. There are eight valves and they are numbered from 1 to 8 starting at the front of the engine. Both the inlet and exhaust valves on any particular engine have the same clearance which is given in *Vital Statistics*.

Each valve is fully closed when a particular corresponding one is fully open (ie when the rocker presses it fully down against the spring) and the following table shows the respective sequence.

Valve fully open	Valve to adjust
8	1
6	3
4	5
7	2
1	8
3	6
5	4
2	7

If the order is followed as shown above it will avoid unnecessary turning of the crankshaft. This order can easily be remembered if it is noted that each pair of valve numbers adds up to 9.

Insert a feeler gauge of the correct thickness in each valve rocker gap in turn. If the gap is correct a slight drag will be felt as it is pulled through. If adjustment is necessary, use a tubular box spanner that doesn't foul the rocker arm when fitted over the nut and rotate the nut. To enlarge the gap, turn the nut anti-clockwise. To decrease the gap, turn the nut clockwise.

When all the valves have been checked and adjusted where necessary, refit the rocker cover and associated components in the reverse order of removal. If you're going to go straight ahead with checking the ignition timing (see below), don't bother to refit the distributor cap yet, and keep your crankshaft-turning spanner handy. When you do restart the engine, check for oil leaks at the rocker cover gasket.

3   Clean or renew contact breaker points and lubricate distributor

After a period of time, due to the sparking which occurs across them, the contact breaker points will need cleaning. A build-up occurs on one contact and a small crater appears on the other one; also the electrical resistance of the contacts increases. These things lead to starting problems and a general fall-off of efficiency in the ignition system.

Vauxhall in fact recommend that the contact breaker points be renewed at 6000 mile (10 000 km) intervals, but you may find that cleaning and re-gapping will extend their life to twice that mileage. However, points aren't particularly expensive, and if you're in any doubt about their condition the best idea is to renew them.

The procedure for removing the contact breaker points varies slightly according to the engine size and production date of your Cavalier, as described below. On all models, make sure the ignition is switched off before you start, and wipe the HT leads and distributor cap with a clean rag – it's important that no dirt, oil or water gets inside.

On 1300 models, prise back the two spring clips which secure the distributor cap, and lift away the cap. If you remove the spark plug caps you can move the distributor cap and leads well out of the way, but remember to label the plug leads 1 to 4 if you think you'll have trouble putting them back! Carefully pull off the rotor arm and wipe the metal tip clean. If the arm is cracked, or the metal tip is badly burnt, it should be renewed.

To remove the contact breakers for cleaning or renewal, remove the screw (numbered 2 in the accompanying illustrations) which secures the breaker assembly to the distributor base plate. Lever the spring away from the insulator assembly and disconnect the two wires, noting the arrangement of the terminals and the insulator for correct reassembly. The points can now be lifted away.

On 1600, 1900 and 2000 models with Delco-Remy distributor, the procedure for getting at the points is slightly different. The distributor cover must first be removed by prising apart the press studs; then remove the two screws securing the distributor cap and lift off the cap. Pull off the rotor arm, examining it as described above, and then remove the anti-condensation cover (if fitted) to expose the contact breaker points.

The points can now be removed as described above for 1300 models.

On 1600, 1900 and 2000 models with Bosch distributor, there's no distributor cover or anti-condensation cover to worry about, and the distributor cap is secured by two spring clips as found on 1300 models. The points are slightly different too, being of one-piece construction. To remove them, take out the securing screw, disconnect the feed wire from its tag and lift out the complete assembly.

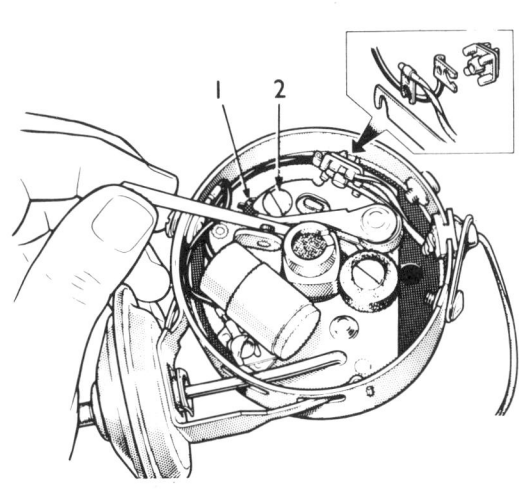

Checking contact breaker points gap – Delco-Remy
distributor

1 Adjusting point   2 Securing screw

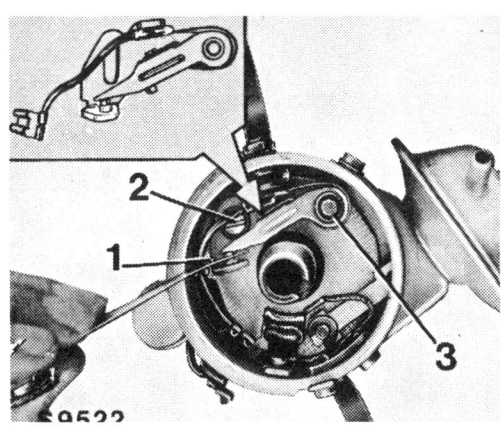

Checking contact breaker points gap – Bosch
distributor

1 Adjusting point   3 Pivot post
2 Securing screw

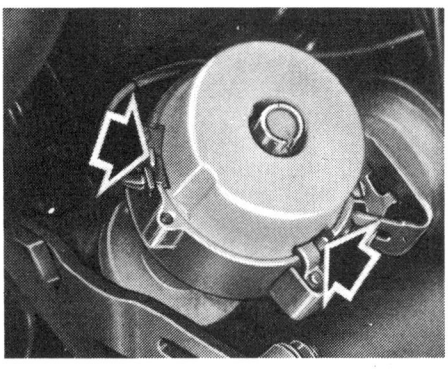

Distributor cap cover. Arrows show press studs

Distributor anti-condensation cover (not fitted to
all models)

Removing the cam lubricating pad (1300 models only)

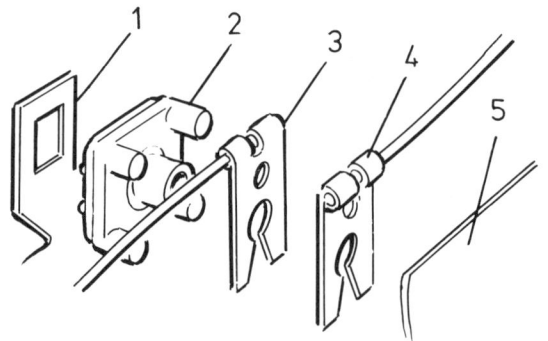

Correct arrangement of distributor insulator post (Delco-Remy)

1 *Fixed contact plate*
2 *Insulator*
3 *Condenser terminal*
4 *LT terminal*
5 *Contact breaker spring*

On all models, examine the contact faces for pitting or burring. If this is severe, the contact breaker assembly must be renewed, but slight imperfections may be removed by rubbing on a fine carborundum stone or fine emery cloth. Take care that metal isn't removed from one edge of the contacts, because when they're fitted they need to be flat and parallel, or very slightly domed so that they touch at their mid points. Make sure that the contact faces are very smooth when they've been rubbed down or they will rapidly burn and wear.

Refitting the points is the reverse sequence to removal, but if you're fitting new points, clean their contact faces first with petrol or methylated spirit. A drop of oil — no more — on the moving arm pivot is also a good idea, and a smear of grease on the cam, or rubbed into the foam lubricating pad if one's fitted will stop the heel of the points wearing too fast. Also apply a few drops of oil to the felt pad in the top of the cam. When refitting the Delco-Remy type points, take care to get the insulator post and the wire tags correctly arranged, otherwise there'll be a baffling lack of response when you try to start the engine.

With the points fitted, the gap between the fixed and moving points must be set. The correct gap is given in *Vital Statistics.* Rotate the crankshaft with the spanner that you used for the purpose when checking the valve clearances until the heel of the moving contact is on one of the peaks of the cam. Slacken the fixed contact securing screw and lever the fixed contact plate with a screwdriver in the slot (numbered 1 in the illustrations) until a feeler blade of the correct thickness is a sliding fit between the point faces. Make sure there's no oil on the feeler blade, or it may contaminate the points. If you do accidentally get oil or grease on the point faces, they can sometimes be cleaned by drawing a piece of thin

cardboard through them a few times; otherwise they'll have to be removed again for cleaning. When you're satisfied that the points are correctly set, fully tighten the securing screw and recheck the gap. Don't refit the rotor arm or distributor cap yet because you'll need them off for the next check ...

4   Check ignition timing

As the contact breaker heel wears, or after a new contact set has been fitted, there may be a slight shift of ignition timing — that's the moment at which the spark occurs. Checking the timing statically (with the engine stopped) is easily done, and we're going to describe this method. If you want a more accurate setting use a stroboscopic timing light (this is dynamic timing); the light will be supplied with operating instructions and you'll find it quite easy to use but, if you haven't got one, dynamic timing's a job for your local Vauxhall dealers.

Ignition timing marks will be found on the crankshaft pulley, with a reference mark on the front part of the engine. On 1300 engines there are two reference marks — the lower one is the ignition timing mark, the upper one indicates top dead centre (TDC). On some early 1600 and 1900 engines the timing marks are at the rear of the engine, concealed by a rubber plug; remove this and you'll see a pointer, which must be aligned with a steel ball pressed into the flywheel to check the timing.

When you've located the timing marks on your engine, rotate the crankshaft until the marks are exactly in line. At this moment the points should just be opening. The easiest way of checking this is to connect a 12 volt test lamp between the moving point and earth, then turn on the ignition. If the lamp

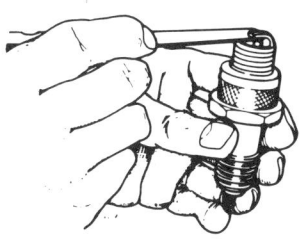

Checking plug gap with feeler gauges

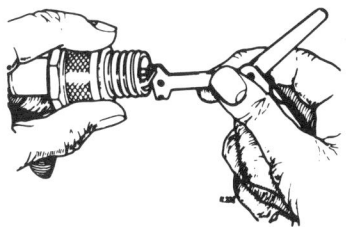

Altering the plug gap. Note use of correct tool.

Spark plug maintenance

White deposits and damaged porcelain insulation indicating overheating

Broken porcelain insulation due to bent central electrode

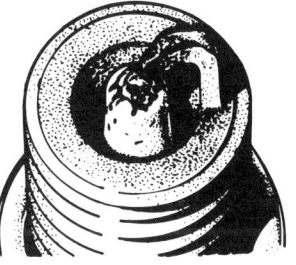

Electrodes burnt away due to wrong heat value or chronic pre-ignition (pinking)

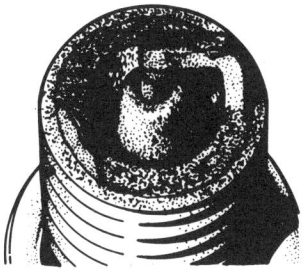

Excessive black deposits caused by over-rich mixture or wrong heat value

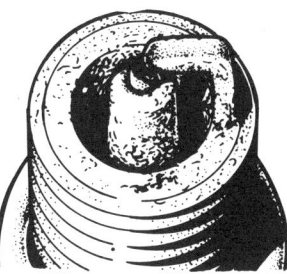

Mild white deposits and electrode burnt indicating too weak a fuel mixture

Plug in sound condition with light greyish brown deposits

Spark plug electrode conditions

comes on the points are open, if it stays out they're closed – so if the timing is correct, the lamp should come on just as the timing marks come into line.

If the lamp comes on too early, the timing is advanced. Slacken the distributor clamp bolt and rotate the whole distributor anti-clockwise slightly until the correct setting is achieved. If the lamp comes on too late, the timing is retarded: in that case rotate the distributor clockwise. In either case, don't forget to retighten the clamp bolt and then recheck the timing just to be on the safe side.

With the static timing correctly set, turn off the ignition and refit the distributor condensation shield (if applicable), the rotor arm, distributor cap and (if fitted) the distributor cover. If you're of a pessimistic turn of mind, refit the plug caps and start the engine just to make sure it still runs – otherwise, leave them off and proceed to ...

Single top brake fluid reservoir

5   Clean spark plugs

Check that there's no dirt around the plug body and cylinder head which might fall into the engine, then remove each plug using the proper size plug spanner. The plugs should be cleaned by a garage equipped with a sand-blasting machine which will remove the deposits far more efficiently than you can with a wire brush, which may damage the surface finish of the insulator around the central electrode and cause misfiring. A spare set of plugs overcomes the inconvenience of having to walk to the garage; in this way you'll always have a spare set ready to use.

Wipe the plug insulators with a petrol-moistened cloth, and check that the screw thread's clean. Check the electrode gap using a feeler gauge of the correct thickness, and if necessary bend the outer electrode to obtain it. Never try to bend the central electrode – all you'll achieve is a broken insulator. When the plugs are clean and reset, check that the seating in the cylinder head is clean and the seating washer's on the plug. Apply a few drops of oil to the plug threads then tighten them down firmly – but no white knuckles or bulging cheeks, you've got to get them out again one day!

With the plugs refitted, put back the plug caps, making sure that they go on in the correct positions.

Double top brake fluid reservoir

6   Check brake fluid level

Two types of brake fluid reservoir have been fitted, one type having a single cap and the other a dual cap. The procedure for checking and topping-up is essentially the same for both types.

Wipe all dirt from around the reservoir cap (caps) – cleanliness is very important here – and unscrew or unclip the cap(s). If the fluid level in the reservoir(s) is below the MAX level, top-up using only clean brake fluid of the specified type. Wipe up any fluid spilt

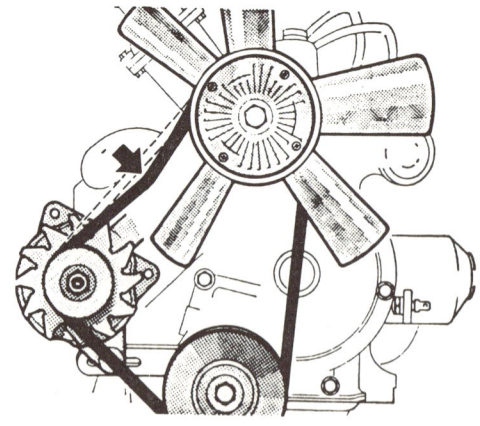

Check fanbelt tension (1300 models)

Check fanbelt tension (1600, 1900 and 2000 models)

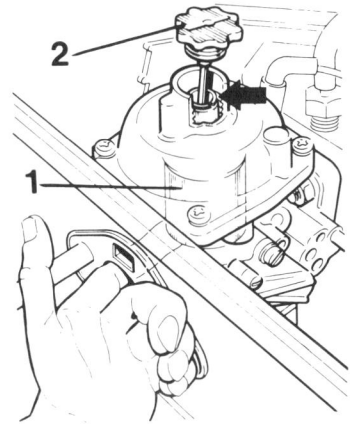

Carburettor hydraulic damper (1300 models only)

1 Air valve   2 Damper cap
Arrow shows hollow guide rod

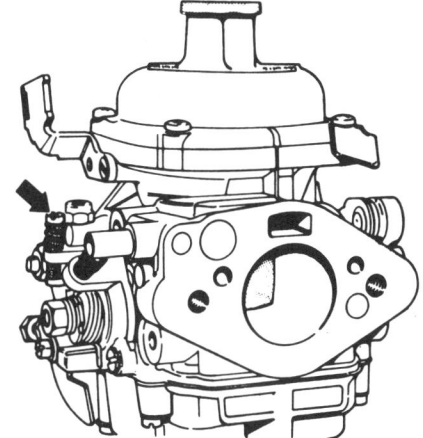

Stromberg carburettor (1300 models). Arrow
shows throttle stop screw

immediately as it's a good paint-stripper, and wash
your hands too as it's poisonous. Refit the reservoir
cap(s) as soon as topping-up is complete.

Frequent need for topping-up the brake fluid
indicates a leak in the system somewhere, which
should be investigated and rectified without delay by
you or your Vauxhall dealer. If the fluid level is
allowed to drop too low the system will have to be
bled, and this again is a job for your dealer unless you
have the necessary skill and information. Full details
are given in the Haynes Owner's Workshop Manual
for your Cavalier.

7 Check condition and tension of fanbelt

It is most important that the fanbelt is in good
condition and correctly adjusted since it drives three
components – the generator, the water pump and of
course the cooling fan. If the belt's too tight, a greater
strain is imposed on the generator and water pump
bearings, shortening their working lives. If the belt's
too loose it will slip, causing overheating and
eventually a flat battery as well. Adjustment is made
by pivoting the generator to adjust the tension of the
belt.

To check the tension, apply thumb pressure mid-
way between the fan and generator pulleys; the
depression should be about $\frac{1}{4}$ in (6 mm). To alter the
tension, loosen the generator pivot mounting bolts
and swing it outwards to increase the tension (using
careful leverage if necessary) or inwards to decrease
it. Provided the bolts haven't been loosened too
much, the generator should retain its position when
they're tightened.

Check the belt for any signs of cracking or fraying
and if it looks at all suspect, renew it. When a new fan
belt's been fitted, recheck the tension after a nominal
mileage as the belt may initially stretch.

8 Top-up carburettor hydraulic damper (1300 models only)

The Stromberg 150CD variable choke carburettor
fitted to 1300 models has a movable piston that is
hydraulically damped by oil, and this oil level must be
checked periodically. To do this first detach the
crankcase ventilation breather hose from the air
cleaner unit, and the air cleaner warm air tube from
the cleaner unit silencer. Disconnect the vacuum
motor tube underneath the air cleaner unit. Unscrew
and remove the six screws retaining the air cleaner
top cover and detach the cover and filter element.

Now unscrew the black plastic cap from the top
of the carburettor and carefully withdraw it and the
hydraulic damper unit which is attached. Insert the
index finger into the carburettor air intake as shown in
the illustration and lift the air valve. The oil level in the
hollow guide rod is now checked and should be 0·30 **51**

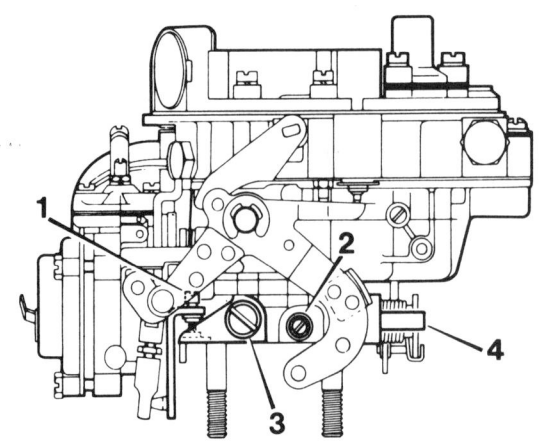

Zenith INAT carburettor

1 Throttle valve adjusting screw
2 Mixture control screw
3 Idling mixture control screw
4 Ignition vacuum control inlet

Solex DIDTA carburettor

1 Throttle valve adjusting screw
2 Mixture control screw
3 Air volume control screw
4 Ignition vacuum control inlet

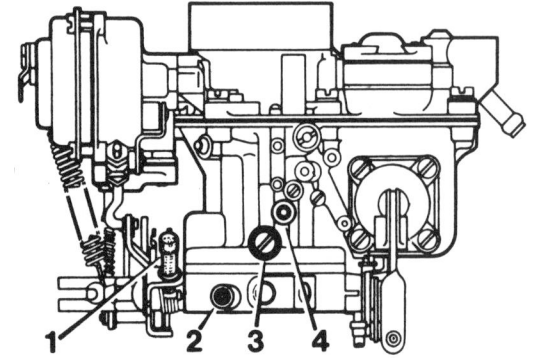

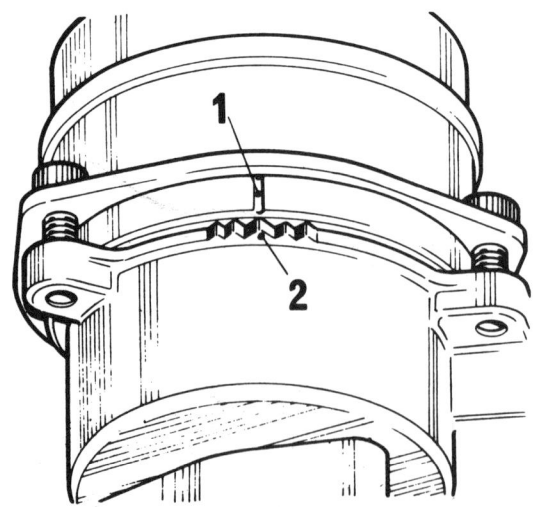

Automatic choke adjustment – Zenith

1 Mark on outer cover
2 Reference notches on main body

in (8 mm) from the top of the hollow guide rod. Top-up if necessary with clean engine oil.

When reassembling, note that the small collar on the hydraulic damper (arrowed) must be re-inserted into the guide rod. This is done by inserting the damper into the guide rod and allowing the air valve to close. Now screw down the plastic cap and lift the air valve again with your finger so that the collar is pressed into the guide rod. This should be further checked to ensure that the collar is correctly located. Unscrew and lift the plastic cap just sufficiently to look down into the hollow guide rod. If the collar isn't seated properly it will rest on top of the rod and will restrict the air valve movement.

The filter element must be refitted with the rubber seal in the downward position. The remainder of the reassembly sequence is the reverse order to dismantling.

Note: *Do not run the engine with the air filter removed – if the engine misfires it could cause a fire in the engine compartment.*

9   Reset idle speed mixture

The carburettor on any car can only be tuned efficiently providing that the associated items such as the ignition timing, distributor contact points and valve clearances are accurately set. Whenever adjustments or checks are to be made on the carburettor the engine must be at its normal operating temperature, and the air cleaner fitted.

If you are satisfied that your carburettor is operating in an economical and satisfactory manner, it is probably best left alone. If you wish to check or make adjustments proceed as follows.

1256 cc engines (Stromberg carburettor)

To adjust the idle speed (ie the engine speed when the foot is off the accelerator) a single throttle stop screw is provided, as shown by the arrow in the illustration. Tightening the screw increases the idle speed whilst unscrewing decreases it. The correct idle speed is between 800 and 850 rpm and this is best measured with a tachometer if available.

If the mixture adjustment is incorrect, a jet adjuster at the base of the carburettor can be reset. However, remember when resetting this that the carburettor performance will be affected throughout its operating range and not just at idle speed. The basic setting of the jet adjustment screw is three turns open. To check this remove the air cleaner cover and element. Insert the index finger into the air intake and hold down the piston. Now screw in the jet adjuster so that it is felt to just touch the bottom of the piston. The jet adjuster must now be unscrewed three complete turns. Refit the air cleaner and run the engine to warm it up, at which point the throttle stop

screw should be adjusted to give a last tickover (idle). Readjust the jet adjustment screw until the engine runs evenly, but note that any adjustment should not have to exceed half a turn either way to achieve this. If the engine fails to run evenly after these adjustments the problem is elsewhere. Two possible causes easily checked are the vacuum tube and connections, which must be in good condition, and the air cleaner element, which must be clean and serviceable.

1584 and 1897 cc engines (Zenith/Solex carburettor)

There is very little in the way of mixture adjustment that may be carried out on fixed choke carburettors. All jet sizes are fixed and are determined by the carburettor and engine manufacturers jointly. The carburettors on all models are expertly set at the factory to achieve optimum fuel metering in conjunction with ignition vacuum advance control. The throttle flap stop screw is then sealed with a plastic cap.

Incorrect adjustment of the throttle stop screw by inexperienced hands could seriously affect the ignition advance timing and the progression system of the carburettor primary barrel. However, minor adjustment to the engine idle speed can be made by the air volume screw and the mixture control screw (see accompanying illustrations).

If automatic transmission is fitted, set the selector lever to the N position. On all cars, run the engine until it reaches operating temperature. Ideally a tachometer should be connected into the ignition system to achieve the correct idling speed which is approximately 800 to 850 rpm. However, the ear can be used to judge when the engine is running smoothly at a sensible idling speed.

Screw the mixture control screw clockwise until the engine begins to 'hunt' or miss, then back it off until the engine again runs smoothly. Adjust the speed of the engine by screwing the air volume screw in, or out, until the optimum speed is obtained.

A certain amount of trial-and-error is required to achieve the correct idling speed, but if satisfactory results cannot be obtained, the best policy is to take the car to your Vauxhall dealer or a tuning specialist who will have the electronic tuning equipment necessary to adjust the carburettor to the optimum setting.

Note: *In the case of automatic transmission, setting the idling speed too high will result in transmission snatch and drag when the D or R positions are initially engaged.*

For automatic choke models a further check should be made to ensure that the mark on the outer choke cover is aligned with the pointer on the inner **53**

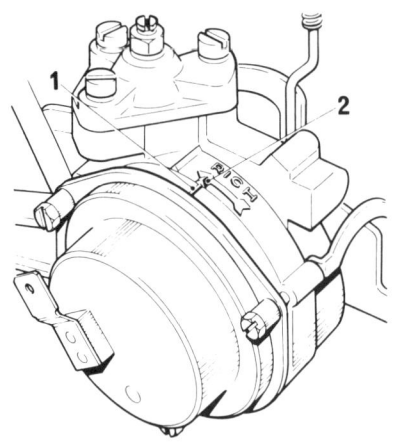

Automatic choke adjustment – Solex

1 Mark on outer cover
2 Inner pointer

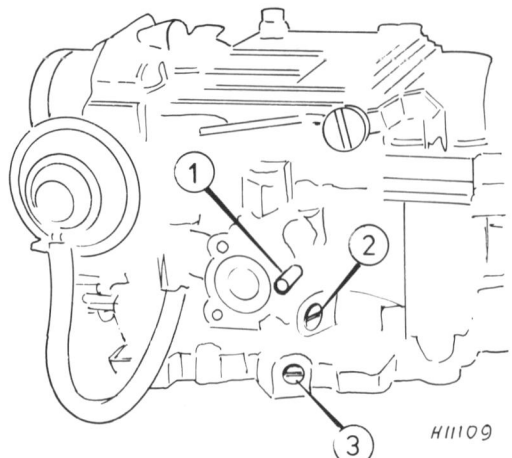

GM Varajet II carburettor fitted to 2000 models

1 Ignition vacuum control inlet
2 Additional idle mixture screw
3 Mixture control screw

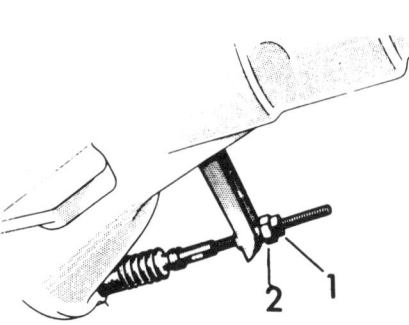

Clutch adjustment – 1300 models

1 Locknut   2 Adjuster

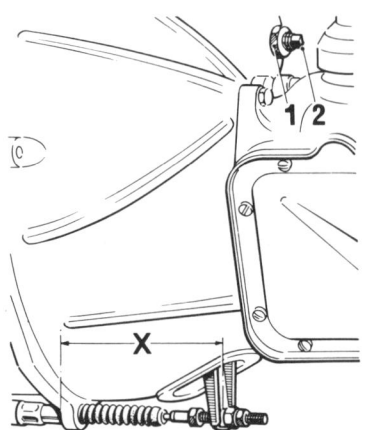

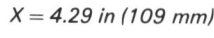

Clutch adjustments – 1600, 1900 and 2000 models

1 Locknut   X = 4.29 in (109 mm)
2 Adjuster

Manual gearbox filler/level plug

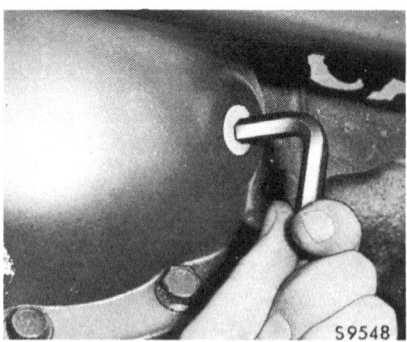

Rear axle filler/level plug

thermostat cover; on Solex carburettors the centre pointer is the correct one.

1979 cc engines (GM Varajet II carburettor)

Fitted to both automatic and manual transmission models, this carburettor is a twin barrel downdraught type. Although the initial idle adjustment is preset in manufacture and sealed with a plastic cap, the idle speed may be further adjusted by resetting the additional mixture screw (A) which will not alter to any great extent the idle speed air/fuel mixture. Only a fine adjustment should be necessary, and should be made with the air cleaner in position and the engine at its normal operating temperature. If the desired results cannot be obtained, see your Vauxhall dealer who will have the necessary test equipment to make any adjustments to the critical level required.

10 Check clutch adjustment

On 1300 models, clutch adjustment is necessary when the clutch pedal height is not the same as that of the brake pedal when both are fully released. Adjustment is made by altering the actuating cable to clutch fork adjustment nuts, as shown in the accompanying illustration. When adjusting, unscrew the locknut and then turn the adjustment nut in the direction required to realign the clutch pedal height with that of the brake pedal. Retighten the locknut whilst holding the adjuster nut in the set position.

On larger-engined models, the clutch should only need adjustment when the warning light comes on, or when a new cable has been fitted. Refer to the accompanying illustration: adjustment is effected by slackening the locknut (1) — you may need a thin spanner and some patience — and turning the pivot bolt (2) until the dimension X is 4·29 in (109 mm). Re-tighten the locknut, operate the clutch a couple of times and check dimension X again.

To check the operation of the clutch wear warning light, release the handbrake, turn on the ignition and raise the clutch pedal with your foot. The clutch warning light should glow; if it does not, and assuming the bulb hasn't blown, the switch or its associated wiring are at fault.

11 Check manual gearbox oil level

On all models a combined filler and oil level plug is fitted to the manual transmission housing and is located on the left-hand side. Access to the plug is from underneath the vehicle so that this is a job best done over a service pit if available. Jacking-up one side won't help as the vehicle must be kept level.

The 1300 models will require a $\frac{3}{8}$ in AF hexagonal wrench whilst the larger engine models will need an 8 mm hexagonal wrench to unscrew the plug.

Clean the plug and the surrounding area before removing it. The oil level on removal should be up to the bottom of the filler plug aperture. If oil needs to be added, make sure you only use new oil of the specified type, and don't overfill. Refit the plug and tighten it. Wipe any spilt oil from the casing.

12 Check rear axle oil level

On all models a combined filler and oil level plug is fitted to the rear axle housing. Clean the plug and surrounding housing area before removing the plug which requires an 8 mm hexagon wrench. The oil level should be up to the bottom of the filler plug aperture. If oil needs to be added use only new oil of the correct grade, and don't overfill. Refit and tighten the filler and wipe any oil spillage from the housing to complete.

13 Check front wheel bearings

Raise the front of the car so that the wheels clear the ground and support it securely. Holding the wheel at the top and bottom edges, try rocking it from side to side and feel for any excessive slackness. A further check can be made by spinning the wheel and holding an adjacent chassis component. If a vibration is felt the bearings should be checked for adjustment or excessive wear.

If adjustment to the bearing is necessary first remove the chrome hub cover (on L models) or the roadwheel (on GL and GLS models) as applicable. Prise off the central dust cap and withdraw the split pin from the stub axle. The castle nut can now be tightened (whilst spinning the wheel) to take up the excess free play. Tighten the nut to a torque of 20 lbf ft 27 Nm) if a torque wrench is available, then unscrew the hub nut until a feeler blade measuring 0·001 to 0·004 in (0·02 to 0·10 mm) can be inserted between the inside face of the nut and the thrust washer to give the correct bearing endfloat. Insert a new split-pin to secure the nut, and refit the dust cap. If roughness or vibration persists after the bearing have been adjusted, they may need renewing; consult your dealer or the Haynes Owner's Workshop Manual for further information. Don't refit the roadwheels or lower the car to the ground yet, because the next task is ...

14 Check brake linings
Disc brakes (front wheels)

The disc brake pad thickness can be checked visually by jacking-up the car at the front and removing each front wheel. The pads can now be inspected between the disc and the caliper body. Brush away any accumulated dust and road dirt, **55**

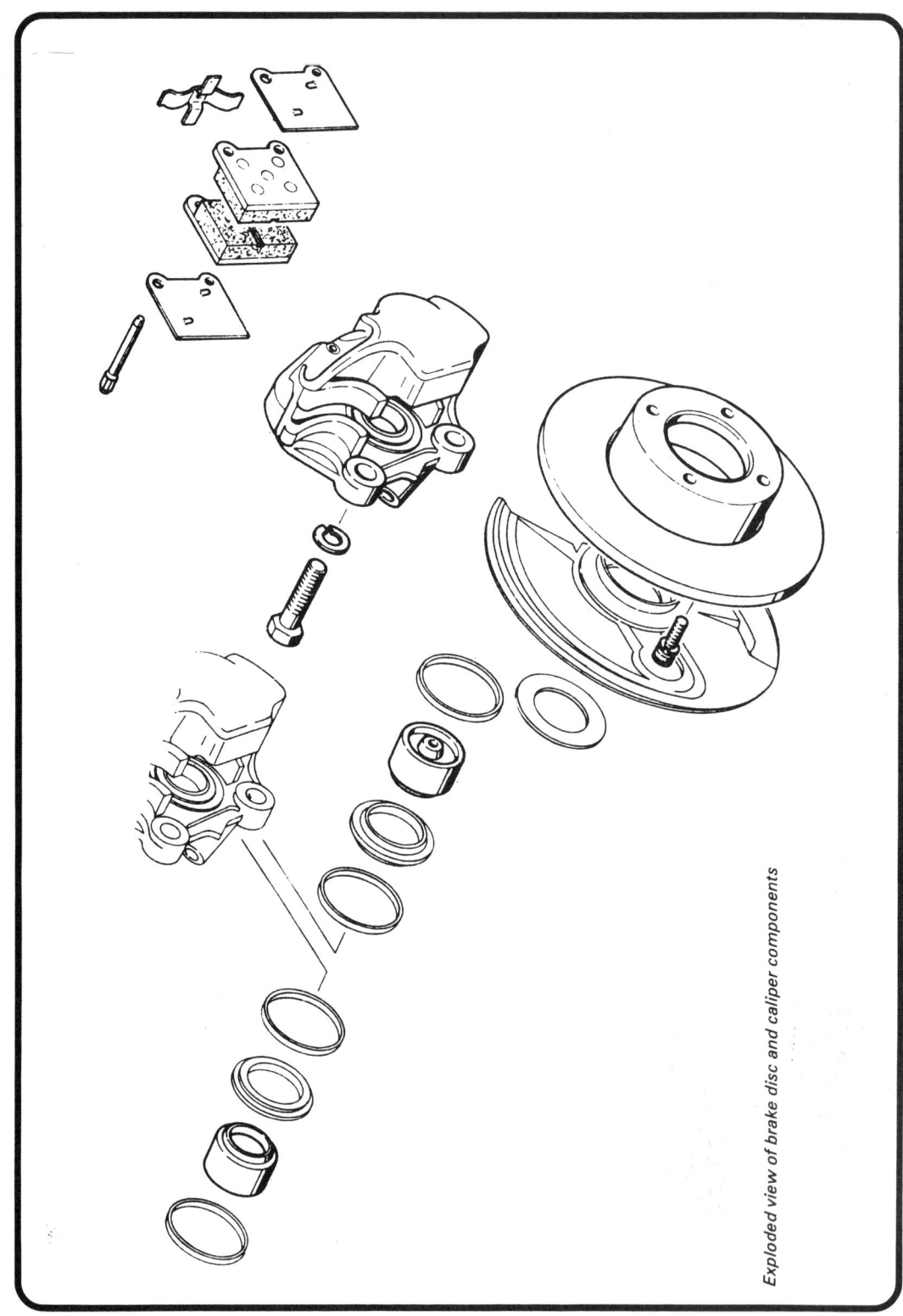

Exploded view of brake disc and caliper components

9488

Checking the wheel bearings for play

taking care not to inhale it as it contains asbestos. Check that the pad thickness is above the minimum specified. If *any* pad is under this thickness they must *all* be renewed.

Renewing the pads isn't a particularly difficult task, so why not have a go yourself? Start by removing the hydraulic fluid reservoir cap(s) and syphon off a small amount of fluid to leave it about $\frac{1}{4}$ in below the normal level mark. This is done to prevent fluid spillage caused by displacement when the caliper pistons are being pressed back into their bores as described below. It isn't essential if you keep an eye on the reservoir during the operation.

Either Girling or ATE brake calipers are fitted. Both types are similar in construction, the main differences being that the pad retaining pins on the ATE calipers are secured by spring collars which should be removed and the pins driven in towards the car using a thin punch. The pad retaining pins on the Girling calipers are secured by spring clips and the pins are driven outwards to remove them.

With the retaining pins removed, withdraw the pads and the anti-squeal shims, noting which way round the shims are fitted for correct refitting. If the shims are distorted or damaged they should be renewed. *Don't press the brake pedal while the pads are removed.*

Inspect the brake disc surface; concentric scores up to 0·020 inch (0·5 mm) deep can be accepted; however, if deeper scores are found, the brake disc must either be skimmed or renewed.

Having removed the pads, wipe the exposed ends of the pistons and the caliper free of dust and road dirt. Press the pistons back into their bores with a piece of wood, being careful that the hydraulic fluid in the reservoir doesn't overflow as you do so. Insert the shims, ensuring that they are the right way round – if there is an arrow it should point in the direction of forward disc rotation – and then insert the new pads.

Refit the location pins and clips. Now press the brake pedal two or three times to centralise the pistons and top-up the brake hydraulic fluid reservoir(s) if necessary. Refit the roadwheels and lower the car to the ground. Remember that the new pads will take a little while to bed in and reach full efficiency.

Drum brakes (rear wheels)

Unlike the front disc brakes which are self-adjusting, the rear drum brakes have to be inspected periodically and readjusted as necessary. To do this, chock the front wheels, jack-up the rear of the car and support on axle stands or similar.

There are twin adjusters to each rear drum assembly and these are located on the inside face of the backplate as shown. A 17 mm ring spanner is needed to turn the adjusters, which are rotated in the direction of the arrows stamped in the backplate to take up the adjustment. The handbrake must be off to perform this function so that the wheels can be spun. When the adjusters are turned sufficiently to make the linings bind slightly, back off the adjuster to just allow the wheel to rotate freely and without binding. This procedure is then repeated on the other adjusters.

After high mileages it will be necessary to fit new brake shoes. To inspect the brake assemblies and linings, remove the roadwheel, and mark the relative position of the drum to the axleshaft at its centre. Remove the spring clamps from the wheel bolts and then back off both shoe adjusters on the inside of the brake backplate to allow the shoes to move inwards off the inside of the drum.

Now ease the drum off the brake assembly to expose the brake shoes, the slave cylinder and the handbrake mechanism. If the drum is sticking to the axleshaft flange, it should be loosened with light hammer strokes on the inside edge of the drum. When refitting the drum it is wise to smear a little medium grease over the contact area of the drum, and axle flange. This measure will help to provide for an easy removal of the brake drum next time.

The brake shoes should be visually inspected. If any have been contaminated with oil or grease – black glazed surface – or if the friction material is less than $\frac{1}{16}$ inch at its thinnest point, both must be renewed. If riveted linings are in place, see whether **57**

Removing brake disc pad retaining pins (ATE type caliper)

Withdraw the pad and shim

Brake shoe retaining pin

Correct installation of the brake shoes on the rear wheel cylinder

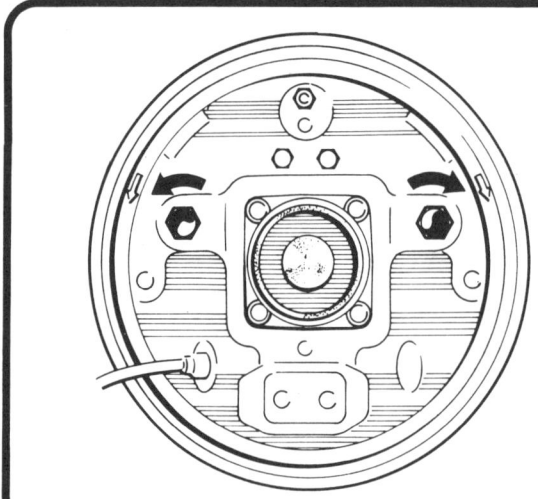

Drum brake adjusters

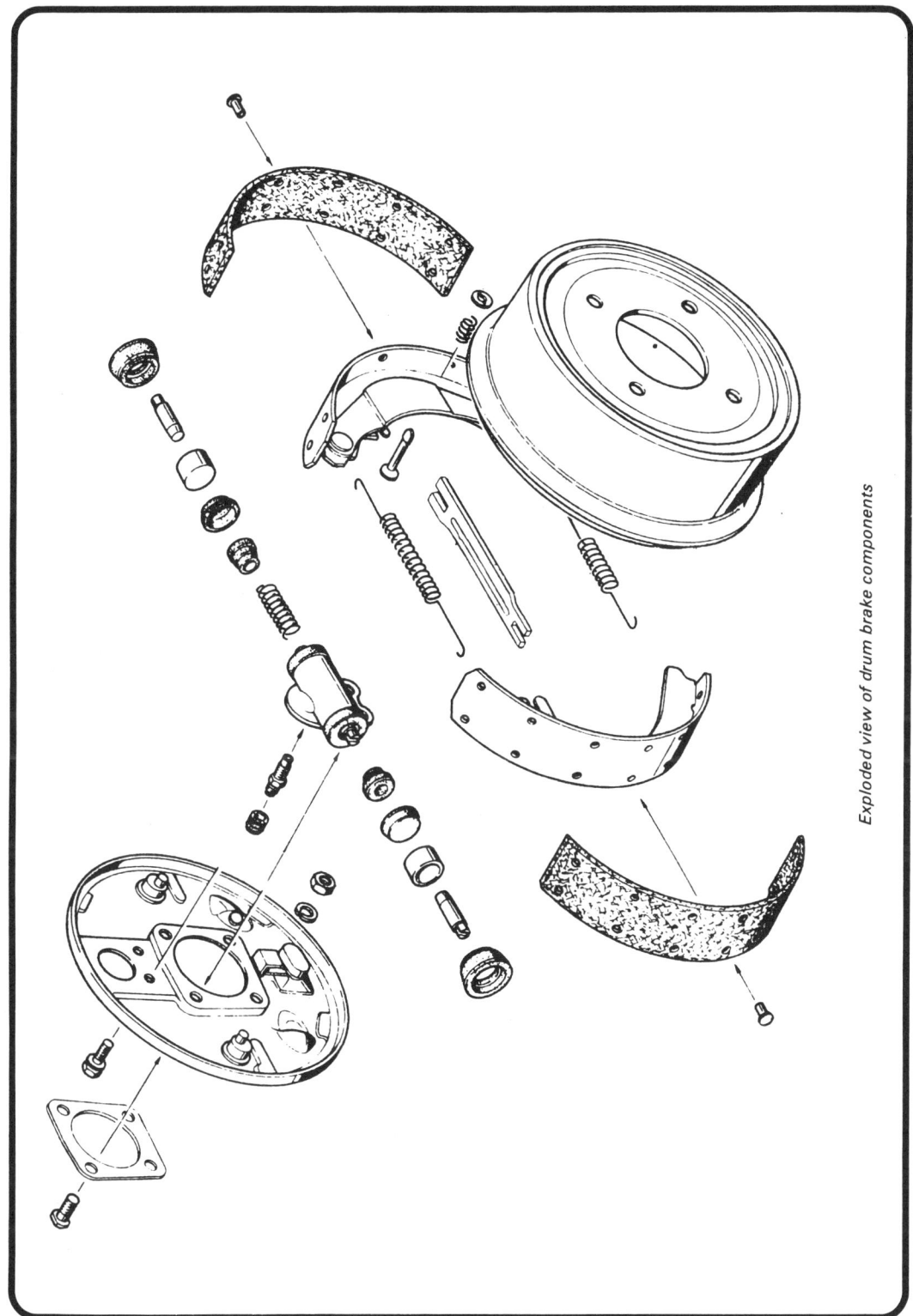

Exploded view of drum brake components

the heads of the rivets are wearing in contact with the drum. The linings must be renewed when the rivet heads do show signs of wear.

If you decide to renew brake shoes, begin by removing the shoe retaining springs in the centre of the shoes. Release the spring retainers by turning them through 90° with a pair of pliers, then lift away the springs, retainers and washers from each shoe. Use a sturdy screwdriver to lever the bottom of each shoe from its anchor and remove the spring from the bottom of the shoes. Now you should be able to remove the forked strip (which is part of the handbrake linkage) and the top spring. Disconnect the handbrake cable from the bottom of the lever attached to the rear shoe.

The old brake shoes can now be lifted away. **Don't press the brake pedal while the shoes are removed,** and if they're going to be off for any length of time, tie a piece of string or thin wire round the pistons in the slave cylinder. The reason is the same in both cases: to prevent the pistons being ejected from the slave cylinder, which would necessitate bleeding the hydraulic system.

Clean all the dust from the brake backplate and drum, using a stiff brush. **Don't inhale the dust** as it is asbestos- based. Check that the slave cylinder isn't wet with leaking brake fluid and that oil isn't leaking into the brake assembly past the axleshaft oil seal. If either condition is noticed, you've an urgent problem on your hands – a failed brake cylinder seal could leave you with no brakes at all, and oil or hydraulic fluid contamination will drastically reduce the efficiency of the linings. Consult your dealer or the Haynes Owner's Workshop Manual.

Smear a trace of brake grease – **not** ordinary grease – onto the ends of the new brake shoes, the brake rubbing surfaces on the backplate, the handbrake lever pivot and the adjuster surfaces. Take care not to get grease on the shoe linings or the slave cylinder rubber boots. Refit the brake shoes in the reverse order to removal; renew the springs as well if they're distorted or weakened. Don't forget to remove the string if you tied some round the slave cylinder! If you have trouble getting the brake drum back on, make sure that the adjusters are backed right off and that the new shoes are properly seated.

With the brake drum refitted, adjust the brake shoes as described above before refitting the wheel – it's easier that way – refit the roadwheel, lower the car to the ground and tighten the wheel nuts.

15 Check the handbrake

When the rear brakes have been adjusted, the handbrake should be checked and should be fully applied within four to five clicks of the ratchet. If more clicks are required, the handbrake cable must be retensioned to take up the stretch in the rod and cable system.

From underneath the car loosen the nuts retaining the cable saddle in position on the rear end of the relay rod, and turn them so as to move the saddle forward on the rod. Re-apply the handbrake and count the notches passed by the hand lever. The hand lever should begin to apply the brakes after the third notch and be fully applied at the fourth or fifth. When the cable saddle has been moved to the correct position, tighten the retaining nuts.

Whilst underneath the car, check the hydraulic brake lines and handbrake rod and cable linkages. Any signs of leaking or chafing of the hydraulic lines must be attended to without delay.

16 General check

Make a general inspection of the engine, transmission and rear axle assemblies, and look for any signs of oil leaks from the joints. Check the tightness of nuts, bolts and fixings. Examine the exhaust system for security and deterioration: If it's leaking, repair or renew the offending section – it can only get worse if left.

Check the fuel lines and their connections. Any leaking or suspect sections must be repaired or renewed.

Lubricate the clutch, throttle, gear change and brake linkages, using grease on the gearshift linkage and clutch cable adjustment nut ball end. Oil the other linkages and at the same time check for excessive play or wear. Renew any suspect components. Oil the door hinges and check links. The door hinges can be lubricated after prising free the sealing plug from the hinge pin at the top. Lubricate the boot lid and bonnet hinges and locks, and the door locks, using a light machine oil.

17 Seats and seat belts

Check the seat fixing and adjustment points for security and signs of corrosion, the seat belts for cuts and fraying, and the inertia reels (where applicable) to ensure that they retract the belts properly. Any damaged seat belts should be renewed without hesitation, since your life or that of someone else could depend on them. If corrosion is found at the fixing points, the advice of a Vauxhall dealer or body repair specialist should be sought.

18 Road test the car

The purpose of the road test is to ensure that everything is running in a satisfactory way and to complete one or two final checks. To start with, find a quiet stretch of road with a straight section of about 150 yards. Before you start testing make sure there's no-one behind. It's very satisfying to know that you've saved a few pounds on maintenance costs by doing the work yourself but it would take the edge of things a bit for another car to career into the back of you, just because its driver hadn't the foresight to realise you were going to stop without notice!

The first point to check is that the brakes are operating properly, especialy if you've removed the pads or shoes for inspection. If any pads have been renewed, remember that they'll need a bit of mileage to 'bed in' and reach full efficiency, so make allowance for this in your driving.

Try the brake immediately you start, just to make sure there's nothing seriously wrong. Then, with the car travelling at about 15 mph, check that all is clear behind, and brake sharply to ensure that the brakes don't pull to one side and that their stopping power is adequate. If any defect is noticed, have it investigated straight away – defective brakes are not something you can live with for long!

Now check the inertia reel safety belts (where fitted) for correct operation: you'll need a front seat passenger for this. Again, with due warning to your passenger, brake sharply from about 15 mph and ensure that both belts lock up immediately.

Continue the test run, with or without your passenger, and listen for any squeaks or rattles that might be present. Wherever possible check the operation of all the instruments and controls, and the car's handling generally. Where automatic transmission is fitted check all the selector lever positions while increasing and decreasing speed as appropriate, not forgetting the 'kick-down' function. Finally, bring the car to rest using the handbrake only, checking that the lever is not excessive.

Have a last look round the engine compartment and underneath, just to check that there are no oil or water leaks.

EVERY 12 000 MILES (20 000 KM) OR 12 MONTHS, WHICHEVER COMES FIRST

(in addition to the items listed in the Weekly and 6000 miles Schedules)
The following additional materials are likely to be needed:

Air filter element, distributor contact breaker points, set of spark plugs, brake servo air filter element, fuel pump cover gasket.

1 Fit new distributor contact breaker points

All the information for this job will be found in the 6000 mile Service Schedule. Wipe the contact faces of the new points with petrol or methylated spirit before fitting.

2 Fit new spark plugs

All the information for this job will be found in the 6000 miles Service Schedule. Make sure the new

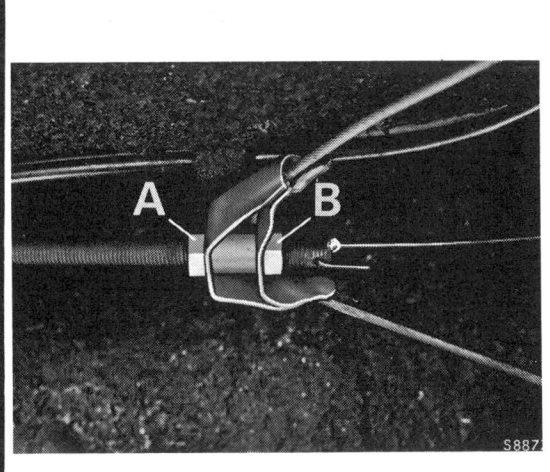

Handbrake cable adjuster

A Front adjuster nut
B Rear adjuster nut

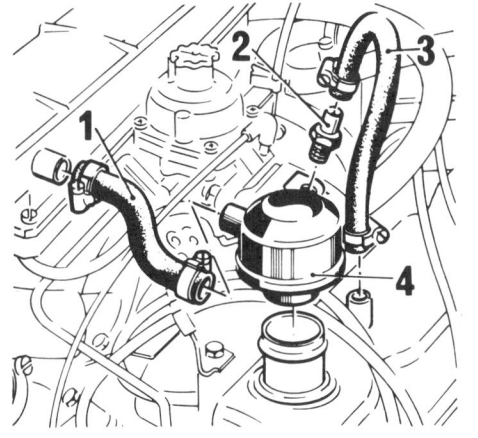

Crankcase ventilation hoses – 1300 models

1 Air cleaner to oil filler hose
2 Hose connector
3 Intake manifold to rocker cover hose
4 Oil filler cap

61

plugs are the correct type for your particular car, and are correctly gapped.

3 Clean crankcase ventailator hoses
1300 models

Refer to the illustration as a guide, and detach the ventilation hoses between the oil filler cap and air filter and the inlet manifold and valve cover. Unscrew and remove the hose connector from the inlet manifold and remove the oil filler cap.

Clean out the hoses – a piece of rag wrapped round a screwdriver blade will do the job – and inspect the hoses for signs of cracks or deterioration. Renew them if suspect.

Clean the hose connector and check that the vent is clear. Clean the gauze filter in the oil filler cap. Don't refit the hoses until you've topped-up the carburettor dashpot (see the 6000 mile Service Schedule) and renewed the air filter element (see below).

1600, 1900 and 2000 models

Detach the crankcase ventilation hoses between the inlet manifold and the rocker cover and rocker cover to carburettor air cleaner. Clean the hoses out as described above and inspect them for any signs of cracking or defects. Renew if necessary and refit the hoses.

4 Renew air cleaner element

The procedure for removing and refitting the 1300 model air cleaner is described in the 6000 mile Service Schedule in the paragraphs dealing with the carburettor hydraulic damper. Before inserting the new filter, wipe clean the filter housing.

On the larger engined models the air filter element is easily removed. Simply unclip the cleaner unit top retaining clips – and on some models, remove the centrally situated retaining nut – and lift the top clear. The element can then be extracted, the container wiped clean and the new element fitted. Check that the seal in the top cover is in good condition – renew it if necessary before refitting the top cover.

5 Check the suspension, steering and shock absorbers

With the car jacked-up and securely supported on axle stands, carefully clean and inspect all the suspension and steering joints. The flexible gaiters must be in good condition, as must the balljoint dirt excluders and rubber suspension bushes. Any that have split or are defective must be renewed.

Check the front and rear shock absorbers. They must be securely mounted and not show any signs of

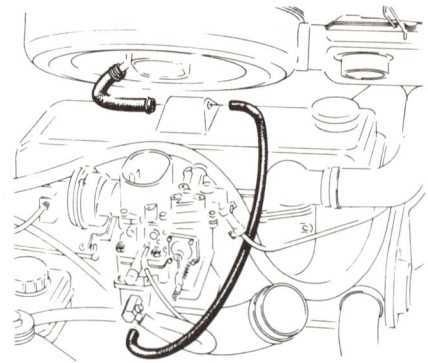

Crankcase ventilation hoses – 1600, 1900 and 2000 models

Air filter element – 2000 models. 1600 and 1900 models are similar

Arrow shows central retaining bolt

Check condition of flexible gaiters and retaining clips (arrowed)

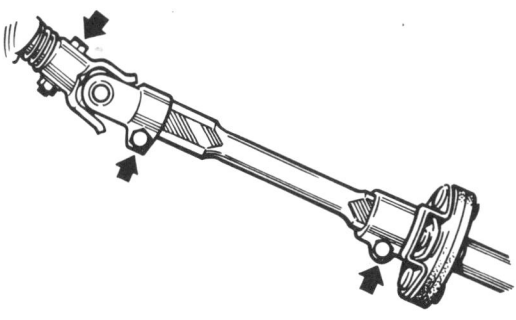

Check security of steering column coupling bolts (arrowed)

Inside headlight adjustment screw

Air filter element with cover removed (1600, 1900 and 2000 models)

leaking. Again, renew if they are defective.

Lower the car from the axle stands and then check the tightness of the various steering and suspension nuts and bolts, including the anti-roll bars, links and Panhard rod assemblies.

Check the steering column flexible coupling for any signs of wear and the coupling bolts for security. The car must be standing on the ground whilst the steering wheel is turned back and forth to enable any wear or damage to be seen. Check the coupling from above, through the engine compartment, and from below the car looking up. If it is worn or damaged in any way, take the car to your Vauxhall dealer for further inspection and if necessary renewal of the affected parts.

Check all other steering and attachment bolts and nuts for security and have your Vauxhall dealer check any joints suspected of being worn.

6   Check the headlight beam alignment setting

As well as checking that the headlights are fully operational, the beam alignment should be checked. This is a task for your Vauxhall agent, who has the necessary optical beam setter to perform this accurately. If a temporary readjustment is to be made, for example to counteract an imbalance in the car loading (towing a trailer, or heavy load in boot), each headlight has two adjustment screws at the rear which are accessible through the engine compartment. One screw adjusts the vertical plane and the other the horizontal plane of the beam. Never set the beams too high or the oncoming traffic will be dazzled and react in the usual way – dazzle you with their headlights!

7   Check operation of brake servo and renew filter if necessary

The servo unit does not normally present any problems, but if it is suspected of malfunction it is easily checked without any special tools. Proceed as follows:

Stop the engine and clear the servo of any vacuum by depressing the brake pedal several times. Once the servo is cleared, keep the brake pedal depressed and start the engine. If the servo unit is in proper working order, the brake pedal should move further downwards, under even foot pressure, due to the effect of the inlet manifold vacuum on the servo diaphragms.

If the brake pedal does not move further downwards the servo system is not operating properly, and the vacuum hoses from the inlet manifold to the servo should be inspected. The vacuum control valve should also be checked. This valve is in the vacuum hose to prevent air flowing into the vacuum side of the servo from the inlet manifold **63**

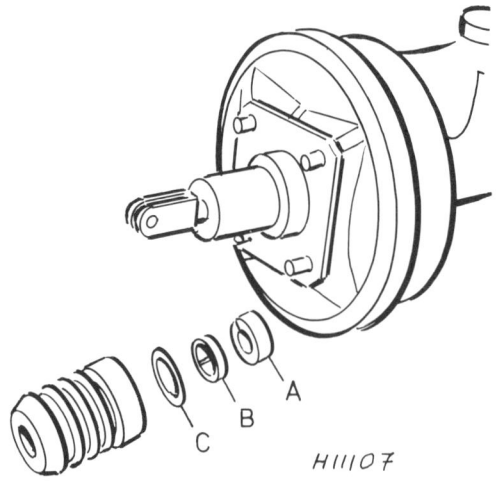

Renewing the brake servo air filter

A *Air filter*
B *Silencer*
C *Retaining ring*

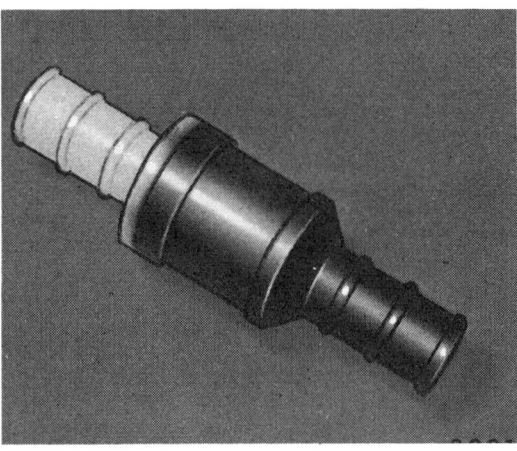

Vacuum control valve

Clean the fuel pump filter (arrowed)

when the engine stops. It is in effect a one way valve.

If the brake servo operates properly in the test, but still gives less effective service on the road, the air filter through which air flows into the servo should be inspected. A dirty filter will limit the formation of a difference in pressure across the servo diaphragm. The servo unit itself cannot be repaired and therefore a complete renewal is necessary if the measures described are not effective.

Air filter renewal

From inside the car, detach the brake pedal from the servo pushrod, then remove the rubber boot over the pushrod housing and air filter. Once the boot has been removed, extract the filter, silencer and retainer from the servo housing bore.

Refitting follows the reversal of the removal procedure. The retainer can be driven into position, with a light soft-faced hammer. The slots in the filter and silencer should be spaced by 180 degrees.

Vacuum control valve

The valve is located in the vacuum hose to prevent air flowing into the servo when the engine stops. It is not repairable and therefore when defective must be renewed. The valve should be located near the inlet manifold union and the arrows on the valve casing should point towards the inlet manifold. Make sure that all the hose clips are properly located and tightened: the system must be airtight.

8 Clean fuel pump filter

The fuel pump fitted to all models contains a wire gauze screen to prevent any foreign bodies drawn from the fuel tank passing through to the carburettor. The particles of dirt trapped by the gauze must be periodically removed. To do this, first disconnect the fuel input pipe from the pump and plug the pipe to stop leakage. Clean the exterior of the pump and then remove the top cover retaining screw and carefully lift the cover clear, together with the nylon distance piece, sealing ring and gauze filter. Clean the filter in petrol and blow through it to clear the mesh holes. When clean, refit the filter and corresponding top cover components. Renew the sealing ring if it is damaged or distorted. When refitting the top cover, don't overtighten the cover retaining screw as you may strip the thread. Reconnect the inlet pipe and then restart the engine and check the pump for any signs of leaks.

9 Check and clean battery

If you've got a hydrometer now's the time to use it to check your battery's specific gravity (SG for short). Assuming that it's fully charged, the SG should be as given in the table, according to the battery temperature. If the battery's been on charge recently, leave it for an hour or two if you can, as it warms up when being charged.

Electrolyte temperature	SG (fully charged)
100°F or 38°C	1·268
90°F or 32°C	1·272
80°F or 27°C	1·276
76°F or 21°C	1·280
60°F or 16°C	1·284
50°F or 10°C	1·288
40°F or 4°C	1·292
30°F or −1·5°C	1·296

If one cell has a low reading it indicates loss of electrolyte (unlikely unless the casing's cracked) or an internal fault. In either case, the end is in insight − prepare to buy a new one before it lets you down.

From time to time corrosion may appear on the battery terminals or on the ends of the main battery leads. Where this has occurred, detach the leads, remove the battery clamping plate and lift out the battery. A solution of warm water and bicarbonate of soda will remove all the corrosion; brush it on to the terminals, making sure that none gets inside. Dip the lead ends straight into the mixture, but remember that too much corrosion will neutralise it so you may need a second mix. Also clean round the battery compartment if corrosion's visible there too. During all this take care that the mixture doesn't get in your eyes, as there's a certain amount of splashing and bubbling as it does its work.

When everything's clean again wipe every part dry with a clean cloth. An underseal type of paint can be used in the battery compartment if there's been corrosion, as this provides a degree of protection. Other parts should be smeared with petroleum jelly before being bolted up. Make sure that everything's covered, but only very lightly. Refit the battery and leads, (fit the earth lead last) smearing a little more petroleum jelly on the lead ends and terminals.

10 Consider the necessity for wheel balancing and steering alignment

Vibrations through the steering are usually caused by the roadwheels being out of balance. Wheel balancing is best carried out by a garage or a tyre specialist, with the wheels on the car, although DIY wheel balancing gadgets are available for 'static' balancing.

If you notice that your tyres are wearing unevenly, the wheel alignment is probably out. Checking and adjustment's a specialist job, so entrust this to a garage. Even if your tyres appear to be wearing evenly it's advisable to have the alignment checked periodically, say every 12 000 miles or once a year.

Some owners like to change their wheels around to even out the tyre wear, and the rotation pattern can include the spare wheel.

However, the latest recommendations with radial tyres are that these should be interchanged only on the same side of the car, ie the direction of rotation should not be reversed as this can cause handling peculiarities. As you'll almost certainly have radial tyres on your Cavalier, you might as well forget about interchanging them; after all, if you do manage to even out the tyre wear it only means you'll have to buy all four new tyres at once instead of just two − and that can be a nasty shock to your bank manager!

EVERY 24 000 MILES (40 000 KM) OR 2 YEARS, WHICHEVER COMES FIRST

(in addition to the items listed in all the previous Service Schedules)
The following additional materials are likely to be needed:

Antifreeze and (where applicable) automatic transmission fluid, automatic transmission oil strainer and gasket, automatic transmission oil pan gasket.

1 Renew cooling system antifreeze

The antifreeze should be renewed every two years and the system flushed through just to make **65**

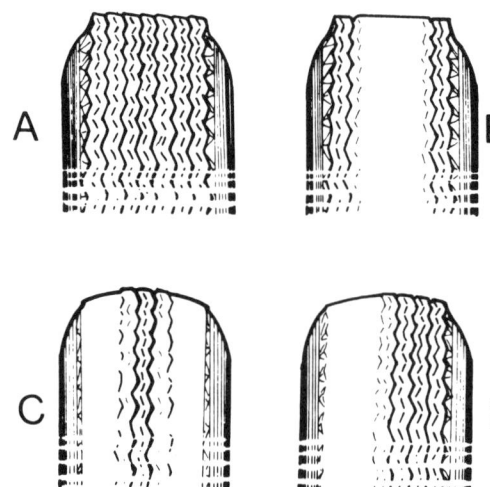

Irregular tyre tread wear patterns and their probable causes

A *'Feathering' due to incorrect toe-in*
B *Over inflation*
C *Under inflation*
D *Wear due to incorrect camber, worn wheel bearings or fast cornering*

sure the job's done properly. To drain the system, place a suitable container at the base of the radiator (something like an old plastic washing-up bowl will do), then slacken the hose clip and remove the hose at the base of the radiator. The coolant will start to flow out and now, if the pressure cap's removed and the heater control moved to the 'Hot' position, will flow out much faster.

When the flow's stopped, remove the engine block drain plug. This is located on the right-hand side of the engine: on 1300 models it's in front of the engine mounting bracket and can be undone with an ordinary spanner. On 1600, 1900 and 2000 models the plug's below the exhaust manifold and requires an 8 mm hexagonal wrench to undo it. The drain hole may be blocked, so probe it gently with a piece of stiff wire. When all the flow from here has stopped too, get a can of water or a hose pipe, and run water through the system to remove any rust particles and sediment that might be present. A proprietary flushing compound can be used if you're suspicious of the system being blocked, but follow the makers' instructions. When you're satisfied that the system's clean, refit the cylinder block drain plug and refit the radiator bottom hose, but leave the heater controls at 'Hot'. It's well worth renewing the cooling system hoses if they're old, perished or cracking – antifreeze has a very searching effect on the hose joints and you don't want to lose it all as soon as you've put it in!

Except in winter, it's not absolutely essential to use antifreeze when refilling the system, but it's preferable at all times because of the corrosion inhibitors which all good antifreeze has. This can stay in the system for two years, and once it's in there's no need to drain it out during the warmer weather. The table below can be used as a guide to how much antifreeze is required.

Antifreeze concentration	Protection to	
%	°C	°F
25	−13	9
33⅓	−19	2
50	−36	−33

Having decided how much you need, the antifreeze can be poured straight into the radiator followed by enough clean water to fill it up. Run the engine at a fast idle to let the mixture circulate; as this happens the level may fall as air locks are dispersed, then will fall quite sharply as the thermostat opens. Finally top up the radiator, if necessary, to the top of the filler neck and replace the cap.

2 Change automatic transmission fluid and renew strainer (where applicable)

Drive the car for at least 5 miles (8 km) before changing the transmission fluid: this will bring any dirt or sludge into suspension in the fluid.

Raise the front of the car onto ramps, or chassis stands; there should be sufficient space underneath the vehicle to gain access to the base of the transmission. A bucket or container to collect about 6 pints (3·4 litres) of oil is required.

Undo the bolts securing the oil pan to the gearbox, remove the oil pan and gasket and collect the oil, but take care – the oil will be hot! Next remove the strainer and its gasket and discard both. Fit a new strainer and gasket. Tighten the strainer screen bolts to 13 – 15 lbf ft (1·8 to 1·9 kgf m) if a torque wrench is available.

Clean the oil pan and when dry and clean, refit to the gearbox using a new gasket. The bolts securing the pan to the box should be tightened to between 7 and 10 lbf ft (0·9 and 1·3 kgf m).

Lower the car back to the ground and fill the transmission, through the filler tube, with approximately 4 to 6 pints (2·2 to 3·4 litres) of transmission fluid. Check the level of oil in the transmission, as described in the Weekly service section. Depending on how cold the transmission fluid is, the level will be lower than when it's hot — if it's stone cold, a level about $\frac{1}{4}$ inch (6 mm) below the ADD mark on the dipstick is equivalent to a full reading when hot. Drive the car for a few miles to warm up the transmission, then recheck level and make sure that there are no fluid leaks.

3   Repack front hub bearings with grease

This task is best left to your Vauxhall dealers as it's beyond the scope of this Handbook, but again if you really want to have a go, details are in the Haynes Owner's Workshop Manual.

4   Renew distributor rotor, condenser and cap

We've attended to most of the things in the ignition system at regular intervals, but the rotor, cap and condenser haven't really been included apart from keeping them clean. To keep the system in perfect tune, these should now be renewed also. The plug leads we've been keeping an eye on, but if your car has the carbon fibre type leads (ie they're not wire inside but black 'string'), these too should be renewed.

Fitting these components is straightforward — the HT leads are retained by small screws or may be simply a push-fit into the distributor cap and the condenser's fixed to the baseplate of the distributor by a single screw on Delco-Remy distributors; on Bosch distributors it's mounted on the side of the distributor and can be removed after disconnecting the LT wires from the coil and the distributor.

EVERY 36 000 MILES (60 000 KM) OR 3 YEARS, WHICHEVER COMES FIRST

(in addition to the items listed in all the previous Service Schedules)

1   Renew brake fluid and all rubber parts in the brake hydraulic system

This is a job for your Vauxhall garage, or for the more enthusiastic owner by following the procedures in the Haynes Owner's Workshop Manual. The reason for doing it is that brake fluid deteriorates after a long period in service, mainly because it's hygroscopic (which means it absorbs moisture from the atmosphere).

Under sustained heavy braking, such as when descending a steep hill, pockets of moisture in the fluid can boil owing to the heat of the brakes; because the vapour is easily compressed it can lead to virtual brake failure, the pedal travelling right to the floor.

The rubber hoses and seals are also subject to deterioration which could lead to fluid leakage — hence the reason for renewing them. Don't neglect this job, it's for your safety and everyone else's too.

OTHER REGULAR MAINTENANCE

If you carry out the procedures we've detailed so far, at more or less the prescribed intervals of time or mileage, then you'll have gone a long way towards getting the best out of your Cavalier in terms of both performance and long life.

That's the good news. The other kind is that there are always other areas, not dealt with in regular servicing schedules, where neglect can spell trouble. We reckon a bit of extra time spent on your car at the beginning and end of the winter will be repaid in terms of peace of mind and prevention of trouble. The suggested attentions which follow have been divided into Spring and Autumn sections — but there's nothing to prevent your doing them more frequently if you like!

SPRING

We've put this one first as it is less depressing than autumn — though there's probably more work involved.

Underside of car

In spring, we venture to suggest, the owner's fancy lightly turns to thoughts of cleaning off all the accumulated muck of winter from underneath the car. Without a shadow of doubt, the best time to clean underneath is the worst time from the discomfort point of view — that is, when the car's been driven in the wet and all the dirt's nicely softened up. So let's talk first about the easier way out — steam cleaning or pressure washing. These are DIY jobs, and can only be body repair jobs. You may feel that this method's unnecessarily expensive, but it's generally preferable to grovelling about underneath and getting filthy and uncomfortable doing it yourself. However, for the owner who really wants to do it by hand, here goes ...

You'll need paraffin or a water-soluble solvent water, (and preferably a hose), a wire brush, a scraper and a stiff-bristle brush. If you think the car floor may leak, remove the carpets or they'll get wet; this will also help pinpoint the places where the water's getting in.

To start with, jack the car up as high as possible, **67**

preferably at one side or one end. For your own safety, support it on ramps or concrete or wooden blocks and chock the wheels which are on the ground. Unless both rear wheels are raised, also apply the handbrake, and engage first or reverse gear.

Now get underneath (you've put if off as long as you can!) and cover the brake discs and calipers with polythene bags to stop mud and water getting into them. Next loosen any encrusted dirt and, working from one end or one side, scrape or brush this away. The paraffin or solvent can be used where there's oil contamination. After all the brushing and scraping, a final wash down with the hose will remove the last of the dirt and mud.

You can now check for leaks in the floor, if you find any, dry the area carefully then use a mastic type sealer to plug the offending gap. Hollow sections of doors and bodywork can be sprayed or brush painted with a rust inhibitor to provide some extra protection. If there are any signs of the underseal breaking away, this is a good opportunity to patch it up. Undersealing paint's available in spray cans or tins from accessory shops; one small point about putting the stuff on though, and that's to make sure the area is clean and dry, otherwise you're wasting your time.

While you're underneath, have a good look round for signs of rusting. Likely places are body sills, floor panels and chassis box sections, and if you find any have a word with your local Vauxhall man or body repair shop before things get too bad.

Bodywork

This too will have suffered from all the muck and salt that's around during the winter, and there's no better time to wash it thoroughly and check for stone chips and rust spots. You're bound to find some, despite the regular washing you've given the car – or meant to – throughout the winter. Treat as for rusty scratches (see *Body Beautiful*).

After the touch-up paint's thoroughly hardened, it's worth giving the car a good polish to prepare it for the long, hot summer ahead (well, there's no harm in hoping!). If you're feeling really energetic you could do the interior as well, but the most important cleaning jobs are now done.

Air cleaner intake (1600 and 1900 models)

Move the air cleaner flap lever from the WINTER to the SUMMER position – this operates a flap valve, which in the WINTER position allows a supply of warm air to be drawn into the carburettor to improve engine performance in cold conditions. Now, with any luck, this isn't necessary for a few months. On 1300 and 2000 models the air intake adjusts itself automatically according to temperature.

AUTUMN

With winter on the way, your car's electrical system is going to take much more of a beating than it has during the last few months. Now – and not on a dark night miles from anywhere in a snowstorm – is the time to check the vital components. Where other Sections are referred to in brackets, the detailed procedure's described there.

Battery

Ensure that this is topped up correctly *(Weekly Schedule, Item 4)*

Check and clean as necessary *(12 000 mile Schedule, Item 9)*

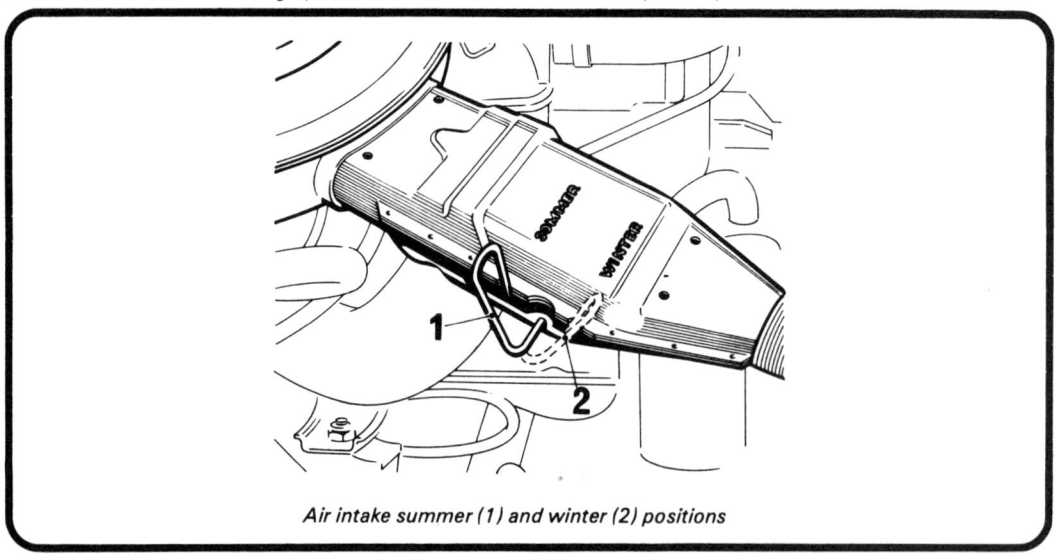

Air intake summer (1) and winter (2) positions

Fanbelt

Check and adjust or renew as necessary *(6000 mile Schedule, Item 7)*

Lights

Check operation *(Weekly Schedule, Item 7)*. Renew any failed bulbs *(In an Emergency)* or check for faults as necessary *(Troubleshooter 6)*

Wipers/Washers

These are going to get a lot of use, so check the wiper arms and blades

Top-up washer reservoir *(Weekly Schedule, Item 5)* and check operation

Cooling system

Check all hoses. Drain, flush and refill system with new antifreeze mixture if necessary *(24 000 mile Schedule, Item 1)*

Carburettor air intake

Reset to Winter position (see *Spring section)*

Tyres

Check tread and condition *(Weekly Schedule,* *Item 3)*. Remember that you may well be driving in slippery conditions

Bodywork

Finally, if you've got any energy left, wash the car and polish it thoroughly to help protect the paint against the winter elements

Aerosol products

When the weather's damp and foggy it plays havoc with the ignition system even though you've taken the trouble to keep everything up together. Aerosol cans of special spray-on water-dispersant chemical are available which, when applied to the spark plug caps, HT leads, distributor cap, coil and battery terminals will instantly dry out the components. Other aerosol products are available which, when sprayed on, form a thin plastic film which seals out condensation, water, petrol and oil. When applying this type of product to the battery and ignition system it's absolutely essential to ensure the areas to be treated are clean and dry.

A can of windscreen de-icer and a scraper for getting snow off the windscreen should complete your preparations for winter.

Body Beautiful

If you've bought this book intending to do all the routine servicing of your car yourself, then you'll surely want to keep the bodywork and inside of the car looking good too. And for anyone who doesn't here's how to do it anyway ...

It's always a good idea to clean the interior first; this way you won't get the dust all over your nicely polished exterior – or the car's! Begin by removing all the contents, not forgetting the odds and ends in the pockets and glovebox. Then take out all the mats and carpets, which should be shaken and brushed, or better still vacuum-cleaned. If they need further cleaning this can be done with a carpet shampoo, but let them dry thoroughly before you put them back. Any underfelt should be taken out and shaken, too, but don't try washing this or it may end up in rather more pieces than you started with.

If the carpets should just happen to be in such a bad state of decay that they don't merit cleaning, why not get yourself a decent set of replacements? You can get kits tailored for your particular model from specialist firms, and they're quite reasonably priced.

The inside of the car can now be cleaned with a brush and dustpan, or again preferably a vacuum-cleaner. If the flex on the Hoover won't stretch to the car (and the car won't squeeze through the front door!) it might be worth thinking about investing in one of the small 12 volt hand vacuums which can be attached to your car battery – your accessory shop can probably show you one.

Seat and trim materials can be wiped over with warm water containing a little washing-up liquid, but for best results (particularly if they're very dirty) use one of the proprietary upholstery cleaners such as Decosol, which are specially made for the job. An old nail brush will help to remove ingrained marks, but don't splash too much water about and do wipe the surfaces dry afterwards with a clean cloth, leaving the windows open to speed up drying. The carpets can be put back when they're quite dry, making sure they're properly fitted around the controls etc.

You have to be careful about cleaning car windows, especially the windscreen, with some household products as these can leave a smeary film. Water containing a few drops of ammonia is probably best, but any stubborn marks and smears can be removed with methylated spirit; finish of) with a chamois leather squeezed as dry as possible.

Just in case you should think that's it, there's still the boot to be dealt with. Take out that collection of junk that seems to have grown every time you open the lid, and get busy with brush or vacuum cleaner again. While you're at it, if you must carry all that stuff around, now's the time to try and stow it so it doesn't rattle any more!

Now you can pause for a moment – make a well earned cup of tea perhaps – and take a critical look at the interior. Are there any nicks or tears in the seats or other trim? Is the headlining drooping or peeling? Some excellent products can now be obtained for repairs such as these. One of the most useful is probably the vinyl repair kit, which comes in various colours and consists of a quantity of 'liquid vinyl' and some sheets of texturing material. The liquid is applied to a split or hole in a plastic seat or piece of trim, smoothed like body filler, and allowed to set. It's then blended into the surrounding area by selecting the best matching pattern from the graining material supplied, placing this over the repair and rubbing with a hot iron; the pattern is then embossed in the repaired area. This type of repair's equally successful, incidentally, on vinyl roofs if your car happens to have one.

For larger splits or tears it may be necessary to cut a piece of matching material from somewhere that doesn't show, apply some suitable adhesive to it and work it under the edges of the tear, pressing these together as neatly as possible once the glue has become tacky enough. Any loose headlining or trim can also be stuck in place – but make sure you get an adhesive that's suitable for PVC or vinyl.

Once you've got the seats in a reasonable state of cleanliness and repair, why not consider seat covers? Like the carpets, they're available from specialist firms to suit your car and are a worthwhile buy in view of the protection they give.

If you use your car regularly and you've got the time and inclination, it should really be washed every week, either by hand (preferably using a hosepipe) or by taking advantage of the local car-wash if there is one. Whichever method you choose (assuming you wash your car at all!) we don't think we need tell you how to do it – but remember it's never a good idea to just wipe over a very dirty car, whether wet or dry; you might as well sandpaper it!

Two or three times a year (even once is better than not at all) a good silicone or wax polish can be used on the paintwork. We don't know which of the many makes you'll use, so we can only recommend you to follow the maker's instructions closely so that you do see a reward for your efforts. Chrome parts are best cleaned with a special chrome cleaner; ordinary metal polish will attack the finish.

If the paint's beginning to lose its gloss or colour, and ordinary polishing doesn't seem to help, it will be worth considering the use of a polish with a mild 'cutting' action to remove what is, in effect, a surface layer of dead paint. Your friendly neighbourhood accessory shop man will advise on a suitable type.

The remainder of this Chapter describes how to keep your car's bodywork and paintwork in good condition by dealing with scratches and more major damage too, as they occur. A number of repair aids and materials are referred to, most of them essential if you're to achieve good results. They should all be available, together with free advice, from good motor accessory shops.

Keeping paintwork up to scratch

With superficial scratches (the sort only other people seem to get) where they don't penetrate down to the metal, you'll be glad to hear that repair can be very simple. Lightly rub the area with a paintwork renovator or a fine cutting paste to remove any loose paint from the scratch and to clean off any polish. Rinse the area with plenty of clean water and allow to dry. Apply touch-up paint to the scratch using a fine brush, and continue to build up the paint by several applications, allowing each to dry, until it's level with the surrounding area. Allow the new paint at least

two weeks to harden (knitting or a crossword puzzle will help to pass the time), then use the paintwork renovator or cutting paste again to blend it into the original. Now a good polish can be used.

For anyone who's as lazy as we are, the easy alternative to painting over a scratch is to use a 'paint transfer', available in packs to match popular car colours. Prepare the affected area in the same way as for touch-up paint , then simply pick a transfer of a suitable size to cover the scratch completely. Hold the transfer against the area and burnish its backing paper, and if you're doing it right you should find it sticks to the car paintwork (rather than your hand), and at the same time frees itself from the backing. The patched area can now be polished to blend it in.

When you've got a scratch that's penetrated right through to the metal, causing rusting, you need a different technique. Use your Scout knife to remove any loose rust from the bottom of the scratch, then paint on a rust-inhibiting paint to prevent it from spreading. You'll probably now need to apply cellulose body stopper paste – use a rubber or nylon applicator or a knife, but don't borrow one from the kitchen as you'll have a job cleaning it!

The paste can be thinned down if necessary using cellulose thinners. Before it hardens, it's a good idea to wrap a piece of smooth cotton rag round the end of your finger, dip it in thinners and quickly sweep it across the filled scratch. This ensures that the area is very slightly hollowed and allows the paint to be built up to the correct level as described earlier.

Dealing with dents

When your car's bodywork gets a deep depression, you'll probably have one too. But there's no reason why even fairly large dents can't be tackled successfully by the D-I-Y owner, especially using the excellent body repair materials now available. So cheer up, and let's see what can be done.

The first step is to try to pull the dented metal out to bring it more or less back to the original level. Don't expect to make a perfect job of this – you won't; the metal has stretched and 'work-hardened' which makes it a virtually impossible job. Try to bring the level up to about $\frac{1}{8}$ inch below the surrounding area; obviously, with shallow dents you can by-pass this bit. If the underside of the dent can be got at, try hammering it out gently from behind using a hammer with a wooden or plastic head. You'll need to hold a fairly heavy hardwood block on the outside of the dent; this absorbs the impact of the hammer blows and helps to stop the metal being dented in the opposite direction!

If you've got a dent in a completely enclosed body section, or there's something else preventing you from getting behind it, a different approach is **71**

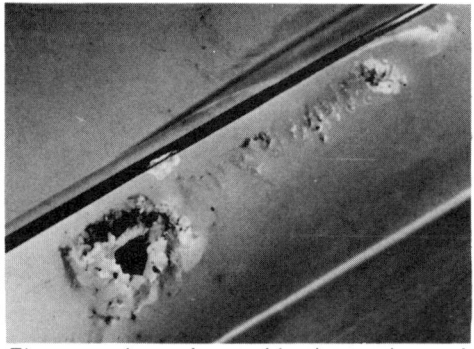

The procedure given with these photos is simplified; more comprehensive instructions will be found in the accompanying text. Typical rust damage is shown here, but the procedure for the repair of dents and gashes is similar.

First remove fittings from the immediate area and then remove loose rust and paint. A wire brush or abrasive disc mounted in a power drill is best, although the job can be done by hand. You need to be very thorough.

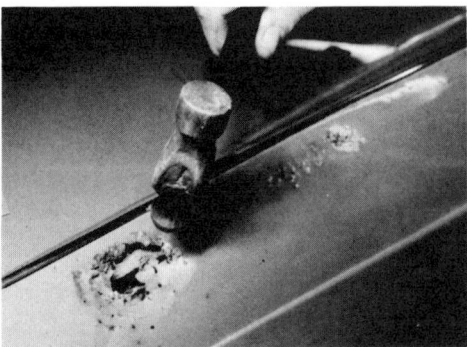

The edges of a hole should be tapped inwards with a hammer to provide a hollow for the filler. Having done this, apply rust inhibitor to the affected area (including the underside where possible) and allow this to dry thoroughly.

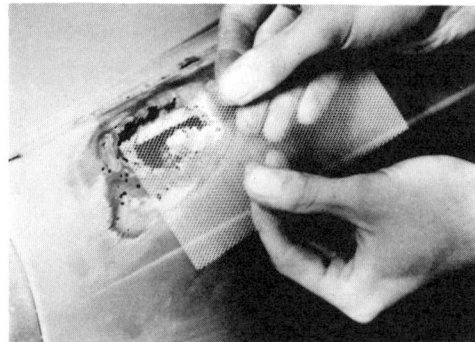

Before attempting to fill larger holes, block them off with suitable material. Metal tape can be used, but the picture shows a piece of aluminium gauze being sized up for use on this hole.

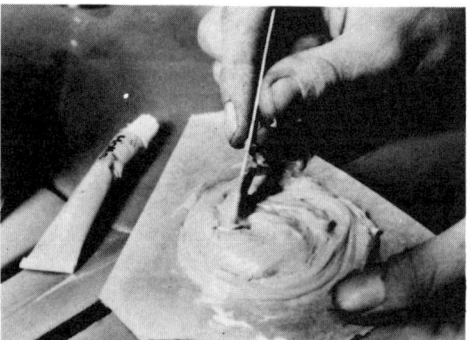

When mixing the body filler, follow the manufacturers' instructions very carefully. Mix thoroughly, don't mix too much at one go, and don't make it up until you're ready to start filling - modern fillers begin to harden very quickly!

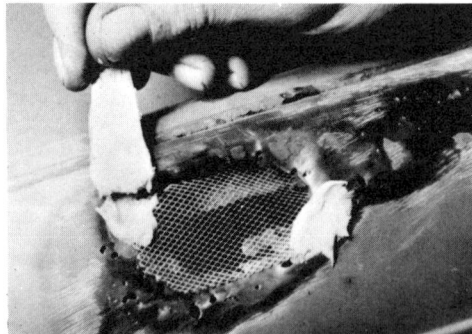

The tape or gauze used for backing up a hole can be secured in position with a few small blobs of filler paste. It's a good idea to mix a very small quantity for this purpose first.

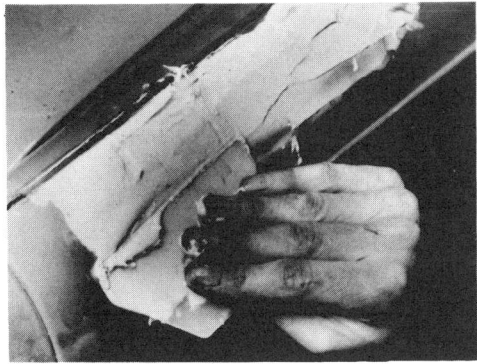

After mixing the filler, apply it quickly with a flexible applicator, following the contours of the body. The filler should be built up in successive thin layers, the final one being just above the level of the surrounding bodywork.

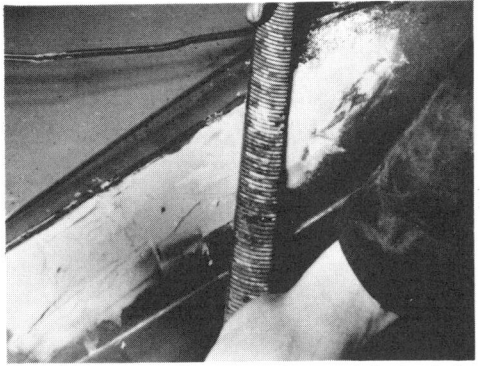

A fairly coarse file or cutting tool is best for removing excess filler and for achieving the initial contour. Care must be taken not to overdo the filing or you'll hollow out the surface and have to fill it again!

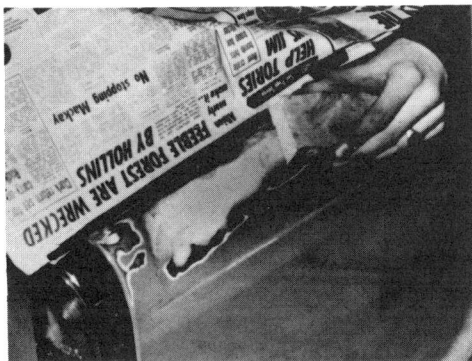

A sanding block will now be needed; this can be made of wood as shown or a purpose-made rubber one can be purchased. Begin shaping the filler by using the block with progressively finer grades of dry abrasive paper, followed by ...

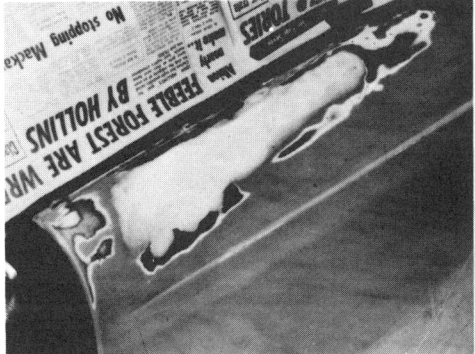

... wet and-dry paper, keeping both the work area and the paper wet. Rubbing down is complete when the filled area is 'feathered' into the surrounding painted areas, as shown; this final stage is achieved with the finest grade paper.

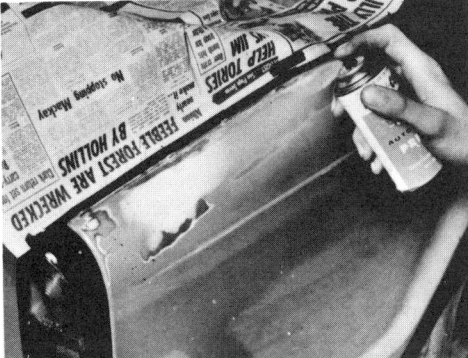

After thorough washing and drying, any necessary masking can be done and a coat of primer applied. Again, build this up with successive thin layers. Once the primer is dry it should be smoothed with very fine wet-and-dry paper.

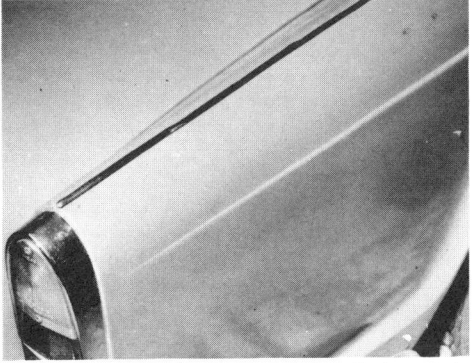

The top coat of paint can now be applied, again in thin layers. Later a mild cutting paste can be used to blend it with the surrounding paint. Finish off with a good quality polish.

needed. Try to screw up enough courage to drill several small holes through the metal in the dent, particularly in the deeper parts. Now screw in several self-tapping screws so that they get a good bite, and either pull on the heads with pliers or wrap some heavy gauge steel wire round them and pull this. Brace yourself in case something gives suddenly or you may dent your own bodywork!

Now to remove the paint from the damaged area. This is best done using a power drill and abrasive disc, but if you've got the time and energy you can use elbow-grease and abrasive paper. Don't forget to remove the paint from an inch or so of the surrounding good paintwork, too, so that everything blends in nicely. Now score the metal surface with a screwdriver or the tang of a file to provide a good key for the filler which you're going to have to apply, in case you didn't know. Now, to finish off the repair, refer to the filling and spraying section at the end of this Chapter.

Rust holes and gashes

If there's any paint left on the affected area, remove it as described above so that you can get a good idea of just how bad the problem is. If there's more rust or fresh air than good metal, now's the time to consider whether a replacement panel would be more appropriate; this is a body shop job beyond the scope of this book.

If things don't seem that bad and you're prepared to have a go at doing the job yourself, remove all the fittings from the surrounding area except those which may help to give a good guide to what the shape should be (e.g. headlamp shells). Now, get a hacksaw blade or a pair of snips and cut out all the loose and badly affected metal. Hammer the edges inwards so that you've got a recessed area to build up on.

Wire brush the edges to remove any powdery rust, then paint over with a rust inhibitor; if you can get to the back, do the same to that. You're now going to fill the hole with something, but unfortunately just anything won't do. The best bets are zinc gauze, aluminium tape or polyurethane foam. The gauze is probably the favourite for a large hole. Cut a piece slightly larger than the hole to be filled, then position it in the hole so that its edges are below the level of the surrounding bodywork. If necessary, hold it in place with a few blobs of filler paste. For small or narrow holes you can use the aluminium tape which is sold by the roll. Pull off a piece and trim to the approximate size and shape required. If there's backing paper, peel it off (it sticks better that way) and place the tape over the hole; if necessary, pieces can be overlapped at the edges. Burnish down the edges of the tape with a file handle or similar to make sure it's firmly adhering to the metal.

Polyurethane foam is best used in hollow body sections but, if you're using this, follow the maker's instructions carefully. When this foam hardens it can be cut back to just below the level of the surrounding bodywork with a hacksaw blade.

With the hole now blocked off, the affected area can be filled and sprayed as follows.

Filling and spraying

Many types of body filler are available, but generally speaking those proprietary kits which contain filler paste (or a filler powder and resin liquid) and a separate hardener are best. You'll also need a flexible plastic or nylon applicator (usually supplied) for putting the mixture on with. Mix up a little of the filler on a piece of board or plastic (those plastic margarine tubs are ideal but do wash out all traces of the contents first!). Read the instructions carefully and don't make up too much at one go. You'll find you have to work fairly fast or the mixture will begin to set, especially if you've been a bit generous with the hardener.

Apply the paste to the prepared hole or dent more or less to the correct level and contour, but don't try to shape it once it's become tacky or it'll pick up on the applicator. Layers should be built up at intervals until the final level's just proud of the surrounding bodywork.

When the filler has fully hardened, use a metal plane or coarse file to remove the excess and obtain the final shape. Then follow with progressively finer grades of wet-or-dry abrasive paper starting with coarse, followed by medium, then fine (some manufacturers give 'grit' grades to their wet-or-dry paper — 40 is the coarsest, 400 the finest). Always wrap the paper round a flat block if you're trying to get a flat surface, and keep it wet by rinsing in clean water or the filler and paint will clog up the abrasive surface.

At this point, the doctored area should be surrounded by a ring of bare metal, encircled by a feathered edge of good paintwork. Rinse it with plenty of clean water to get rid of all the paint and filler dust, and allow it to dry completely.

If you're happy with the surface you've obtained, then you're ready to apply some paint. First spray over the whole area with a light coat of grey primer. This will show up any surface imperfections which may need further treatment, and will also help you get the knack of spraying with an aerosol can before you start on the colour coats. Rub down the surface again, and if necessary use a little body stopper, as described for minor scratches, to fill any small imperfections. Repeat this spray-and-level procedure until you're satisfied with the finish; then wash down again and allow to dry.

The next stage is to apply the finishing coats, but first a word or two about the techniques involved. Paint spraying should be done in a warm, dry, windless, dust-free atmosphere – conditions not very readily available to most of us! You may be able to approach them artificially if you've got a large indoor workshop, but if you have to work outside you'll need to pick the day carefully. If you're working in your garage you'll probably need to 'lay' the dust on the floor by damping it with water.

If the body repair's confined to a small patch, mask off the surrounding area to protect it from paint spray. Bodywork fitting (chrome strips, door handles and the like) will need to be either masked or removed. If you're masking, use genuine masking tape and plenty of newspaper as necessary. Before starting to spray, shake the aerosol can thoroughly; then experiment on something (an old tin or similar will do – not the neighbours' car!) until you feel you can apply the paint smoothly. At the previous stage this wasn't too important, but now you're trying to get the best possible finish.

First cover the repair area with a thick coat of primer – not as one coat, but built up of several thin ones. When this is dry, using the finest wet-or-dry paper, rub down the surface until it's really smooth. Use plenty of water to keep the surface clean; when it's dry, spray on another primer coat and repeat the procedure.

Now for the top coat. Again the idea's to build up the paint thickness by several thin coats. Have a test spray first as this is a different aerosol, then commence spraying in the centre of the repair area. Using a circular motion, work gradually outwards towards the edges until the whole of the repair and about two inches of the surrounding original paint is covered. Remove all the masking material 10 to 15 minutes after you've finished spraying.

Now you can start putting away all the bits and pieces because it'll need about two weeks for the paint to harden completely. After this time, using a paint renovator or a very fine cutting paste, blend the edges of the new paint into the original. Finally, apply a good wax or silicone polish, and hopefully you'll have a repair you're proud to own up to!

Adding 'Pinstripes'

There are various kinds of self-adhesive body decor available for customising your car. Perhaps the neatest and most suitable of the 'add-on' variety are 'Pinstripes', and we've mentioned these here as they may appeal to the owner who wants a cheap and simple way to improve the appearance of his or her car. 'Pinstripes' are an adhesive tape which comes in different widths and colours, and as single or multistripes. Most have a backing paper which is peeled off as the stripe's applied.

When applying any of these self-adhesive tapes, first make sure the paintwork's clean by washing with warm water and a car shampoo or liquid detergent. Next clean up the surface with a very fine cutting paste or paintwork renovator, and wash down again. You can now apply the tape, but follow the directions carefully. Smooth it down with clean rag and, if necessary, prick out any small air bubbles with a pin. Try not to stretch the stripes as you put them on because they'll shrink slightly anyway; and wrap the ends round the panels so that they don't pull away at the edges.

Upholstery painting

If you think the upholstery or interior panelling of your car requires renovating, or maybe you want to improve the colour scheme or make it look more sporty, there are various colours of upholstery paint available in accessory shops. You can also use the paint to cover up repairs, but make sure it's a perfect match or you could make things look worse.

The Personal Touch

On the subject of accessories it's been said that, if somebody makes it, the motorist will buy it. The 'aftermarket' in extras has now grown to enormous proportions, and it can be difficult to sort out the useful and practical items from what, at the other end of the scale, is some undoubted rubbish.

We'd need several volumes to discuss all the various kinds of things you might conceivably buy for your car, and those we have managed to mention can't be gone into in great detail in a book like this. Some time spent browsing around a good motor accessory shop will reveal more than we can here, but nevertheless we hope the suggestions given may prove useful.

All good products will be supplied with general fitting instructions which may or may not require minor modifications to suit your Cavalier. If you're buying secondhand, of course, you may get no instructions at all. The guidelines given here are in no way intended to replace the manufacturer's instructions, and if you're in doubt about fitting a particular item, they're the people to refer to.

Note: *always disconnect the battery before commencing any work involving the electrical system. Fireworks are pretty, but there's a time and place for everything!*

Auxiliary instruments

It would be possible to write a complete book just on auxiliary instruments and how to fit them but,as with other things, you'll normally get pretty good instructions when you buy them. Because there are so many instruments available, we're only going to consider ammeters, battery condition indicators, clocks, oil pressure gauges, tachometers and vacuum gauges.

First of all, even before you've decided what instruments you're going to fit, you've got to think where to fit them. Some instruments such as tachometers can be 'pod' types which are attached to the top of the dash panel.

Sooner or later you're going to have to start drilling some holes somewhere, but this needn't cause any real headaches if it's approached in the right way. Make sure there's nothing behind the panel

before even considering drilling a hole, and that there's enough room to fit the instrument, switch, or whatever, in the space chosen. Any hole which will have a cable or capillary running through it must have a plastic or rubber grommet to prevent the metal chafing through; These grommets can be obtained from DIY accessory or car electrical shops.

When it comes to drilling larger holes for instruments, start off by centre-punching the middle of the area, then use compasses or dividers to mark the hole, allowing a little for clearance (standard instruments are 2 inch/52 mm diameter). It's best to mark another hole inside the first hole, and drill around this line so that the centre part can readily be pushed out; if you're using a $\frac{1}{8}$ in drill the inner circle will need to be $\frac{1}{16}$ in inside the first circle marked. Finish the job off by carefully filing and deburring the hole.

Ammeter

Car manufacturers don't usually fit ammeters as standard equipment these days, and it's not just that they're mean – it's because modern cars, Cavaliers included, are fitted with alternators instead of dynamos. One of the advantages of the alternator is that it can produce twice as much charging current as the old type of generator, but this also means that the ammeter has to be able to register twice the current, and the cable used to connect it up must be very thick to avoid overheating, which could be dangerous, or a voltage drop, which could upset the charging of the battery. For this reason the battery condition indicator

Some of the supplementary instruments and other accessories available from Smiths Industries

(see below) has largely superseded the ammeter. If you must fit an ammeter, though, get one with a −50 to +50 amp scale. The wire used for connecting it up should be at least 84/0·30 (previously designated 84/0·012), and make sure the connections are really secure — just twisting the wires together won't do. The ammeter's connected so that it measures all the current supplied to and drawn from the battery, except for the starting circuit.

After connecting up the ammeter, if it's found to be indicating charge instead of discharge and vice versa, simply reverse the connections at the back of the gauge, but do remember to disconnect the battery lead before doing this.

Battery condition indicator

The battery condition indicator's simply a voltmeter, and as such must be connected to a good earth point on the chassis and to any suitable connection which is live when the ignition switch is ON. For convenience this could be the accessory terminal of the ignition switch, or an ignition-controlled fuse. You won't need heavy cables for the battery condition indicator, 14/0·30 (14/0·012) should be OK, but make sure that the earth polarity's correct.

Clock

Clocks come in many forms, but most types contain semi-conductors. If this means nothing else to you, it means that there's negligible load on the battery and that the polarity's critical if you don't want to cause permanent damage. Connections are much the same as for the battery condition indicator, except that you don't want the clock to stop when the ignition's switched off. Therefore a suitable connecting point should be a fuse which isn't controlled by the ignition switch.

Tachometer

The tachometer (rev counter) is one instrument that's available in larger sizes than the others (80 mm instead of 52 mm, although the smaller sizes can be obtained). Most are positive or negative earth, but

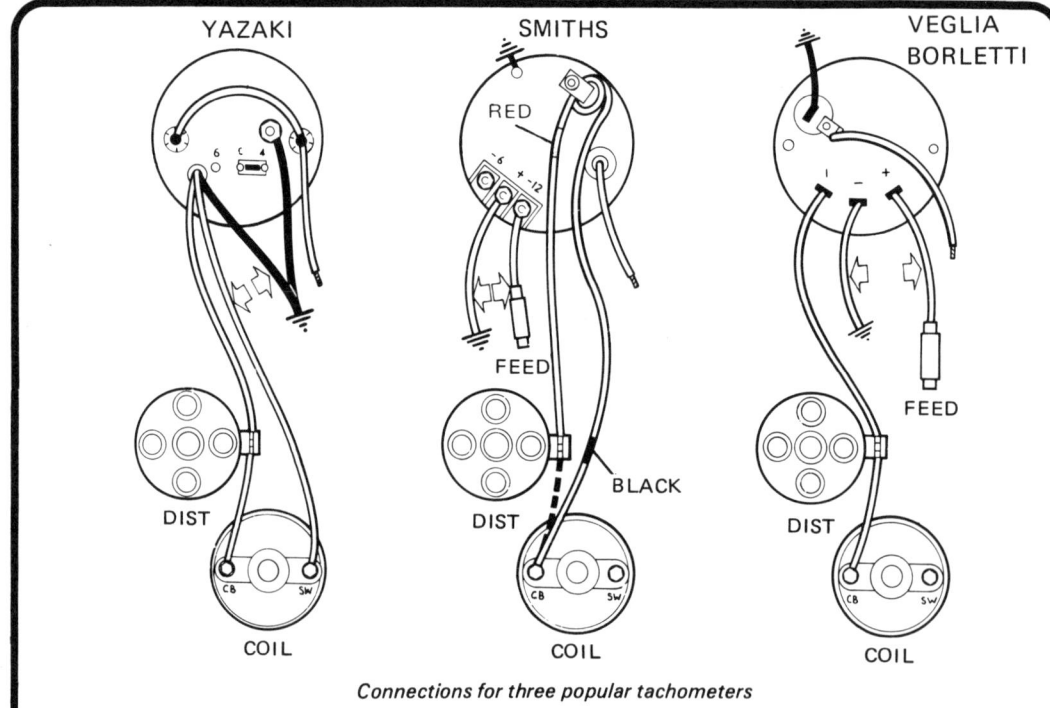

Connections for three popular tachometers

YAZAKI: negative earth shown

SMITHS: Positive earth shown, the dotted connection must be removed when the tachometer is connected. Reverse arrowed wires to change polarity

VEGLIA BORLETTI: Negative earth shown

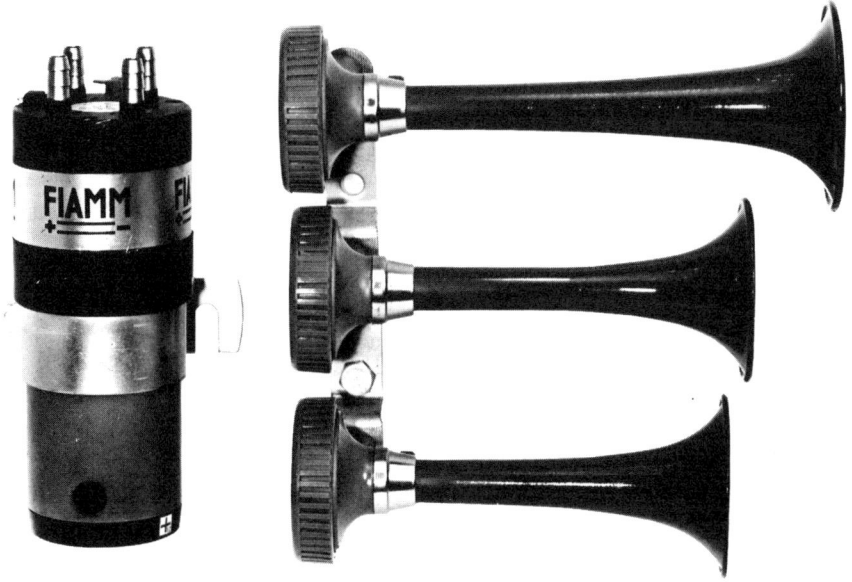

Fiamm 'trio' air horns

you must connect them up correctly. If you should pick up a secondhand one, connections for the most common types are shown in the illustrations. Note that with the Smiths type, the distributor-to-coil LT lead is removed; also note the sleeve colours on the main white lead. Use a 14/0·30 (14/0·012) cable size.

Oil pressure gauge

There are two main types of oil pressure gauge, the capillary type and the electrical sender type. For the capillary type you can use a tee-piece and tap into the oil pressure switch tapping which is screwed into the oil filter housing. For the electric type you've got to connect up feed wires but the manufacturer's instructions should clearly explain the details.

Vacuum gauge (performance gauge or fuel consumption gauge)

This is simply a suction (negative pressure) gauge which screws into a tapping on the inlet manifold, with a flexible pipe for the meter. Most types are supplied with a small clamp which is used to restrict the pulsating flow in the flexible pipe; it's tightened until the smoothest possible gauge indication is obtained.

Warning devices

Air horns

Air horns are marketed by several companies as a DIY installation kit comprising the horns themselves, a compressor unit, a relay, plastic piping and electrical cable. What you've obviously got to do is mount the horns reasonably near the compressor, and the compressor reasonably near the relay, or the connections just won't reach. It's normal for the manufacturers to specify a certain way up for the compressor to be mounted, but there shouldn't be any other problems. You'll need to make sure that the electrical connections are as per the maker's instructions for the relay and compressor, and decide whether you want to use the air horns in conjunction with, or in place of, the original car horn. If you have to connect into existing wiring, make sure that the connections are well made and, if these involve soldering, don't forget to insulate any soldered joints.

Child safety seats and harness

A lot has been said and written in recent years about the use of seat belts for front seat passengers, and more recently there's been an increasing interest **79**

KL's 'Jeenay' child safety seat

in the various special rear seats and safety restraints now available for young children. It's very difficult to give any precise instructions for fitting these, because there are so many types around, but what you must be careful about is ensuring that you buy a BSI-approved type.

Most types have a pair of straps at the front edge which need to be attached to the rear seat pan at the back of the squab, and a further pair of straps that fit over the back of the car seat for attachment to the rear parcel shelf (or the floor or wheel arch with estate cars). Take very careful note of the manufacturer's instructions; they require the anchorages to be a certain distance apart, and will probably also require reinforcing plates to be used. Before starting to drill holes for the mountings, make sure the underside or rear of the panel's clear of obstruction, pipes or any other components.

Auxiliary lamps

When auxiliary lamps are fitted, not only must you fit them in a suitable place on the car, but you must also meet certain legal requirements; where these apply we've attempted to give some guidelines.

In addition to the actual lamps themselves, we have to think of the switch (not normally difficult because many small switch panels are available), fusing, cable sizes and whether relays are necessary.

Spot and front fog lamps

It's illegal to mount these with the lower edge of the illuminating surface more than 1200 mm (47·24 in) from the ground. Any lamps that are mounted with this lower edge less than 500 mm (19·69 in) above the ground may only be used in fog or falling snow. In conditions where the law requires headlamps to be used, eg at night on an unlit road, a single lamp may be used only in conjunction with the headlamps. In these conditions the lamps must always be mounted and used in pairs (two fog, two spot or one of each) if they're to be used independently of the headlamps.

Their outer edges must be within 400 mm (15·75 in) of the edge of the car and (in the case of vehicles first used before January 1, 1971 only) their inner edges must be not less than 350 mm (13·78 in) apart. If they're used as spotlamps, they should conform to the normal anti-dazzle requirements, eg by wiring them so that they go out when the headlamps are dipped, or by angling them slightly downwards.

Choose the lamps carefully, and if possible match the lamp styles. There are many good types on sale, so it you're not sure what you want ask for advice. The actual mounting is not too difficult; they can either be fitted to a bumper bracket or attached by a separate bracket to the front grille.

To prevent overloading of the existing wiring, a relay should be used (the Lucas 6RA type, part No 33213, is suitable). This is connected through the switch from the existing headlamp circuit to one of the relay 'coil' terminals, the other going to a good earth point. The lamp wires then go to one of the relay 'contact' terminals, with the other terminal being connected either to the battery or the battery connection at the starter solenoid, via a line fuse. The fuse rating will depend on the lamp manufacturer's recommendations, but will probably be about 20 amps for a pair of lamps.

Rear fog lamps

These can often be mounted in much the same way as reversing lamps, although bumper-mounting types are popular, in fact some lamps serve a dual function in having a clear lens for reversing and a red snap-on lens for the warning lamp.

Under the Road Vehicles (Rear Fog Lamps) Regulations 1978, the fitting of at least one rear fog lamp will become compulsory on cars manufactured on or after October 1, 1979 and first used on or after April 1, 1980. These same regulations lay down specific rules on the use and positioning of such lamps.

Either one or two lamps may be fitted. If only one is used, it must be on the centre line or to the offside

without rear fog lamp

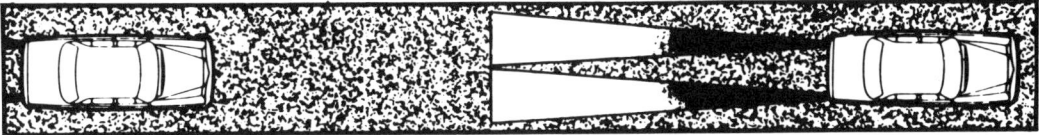

with rear fog lamp

Diagram showing the benefits of fitting a rear fog lamp

of the car, and at least 100 mm (3·94 in) from the nearest brake light. No rear fog lamp is to be illuminated by the braking system of the car. The rear fog lamp switch must have a warning light to indicate to the driver when the lamps are switched on, and this switch must be wired in such a way that the rear fog lamp(s) cannot be used without either headlights, sidelights or front fog lamps also being on.

Any rear fog lamp fitted to a car manufactured from October 1, 1979 must also bear the appropriate 'E-mark' signifying conformity with EEC standards. If your car was manufactured prior to that date then you *nned* not fit rear fog lamps at all; but if you do (and it obviously makes sense to do so) they must comply with the above regulations concerning positioning and independence of the brake lights.

Conditions requiring the use of rear fog lamps obviously also call for headlamps and/or front fog lamps. While front fog lamps may be used only in fog or falling snow, rear fog lamps are to be permitted in conditions of 'poor visibility' when only headlamps may be allowable at the front. It is suggested, therefore, that if you fit rear fog lamps they're wired using a relay, the actuating circuit of which is operated by the dipped headlamps circuit (ie the supply to terminal 'W1' in our relay diagram would come from a dipped headlamp circuit connection).

The cable from the switch should be run through the car floor if possible and under the carpet, but don't forget to use grommets or the holes which you've drilled will cut through the cable insulation. An in-line fuse will be needed, probably about 10 amps rating, but it will depend on the actual lamps fitted.

Anti-theft devices

There are three main categories of car thieves – those people who want your car either as a complete item or for the major mechanical and body parts; those who are out for a joy-ride; and those who merely want the contents. With any type of thief it makes sense to do what you can to prevent someone from wanting to get in; don't leave valuables lying about, don't leave the car unlocked and, if it's parked at home, put it in a locked garage if possible. But if a car thief decides he wants your particular car, statistically he's got a pretty good chance of getting it!

All Cavaliers have a steering column lock which is a very effective protection against a car being driven away, but it still makes sense to have a good burglar alarm fitted. Many types are available, and many of these are wired into door courtesy light switches or hidden switches beneath the seats. Most types are wired into the car horn circuit but separate horns and bells are available; the more unconventional it is (whilst still being reliable!) the better. Don't put hidden switches in the first place you think of – it might be the first place the thief thinks of too.

Some anti-theft devices are activated by the movement caused through somebody trying to get into the car (and occasionally by an innocent passer-by!). Some not only sound alarms, but also earth the ignition circuit, other devices simply mechanically lock together the steering wheel and brake pedal. Have a look round the accessory shops and see what suits your car, your pocket and the degree of protection required.

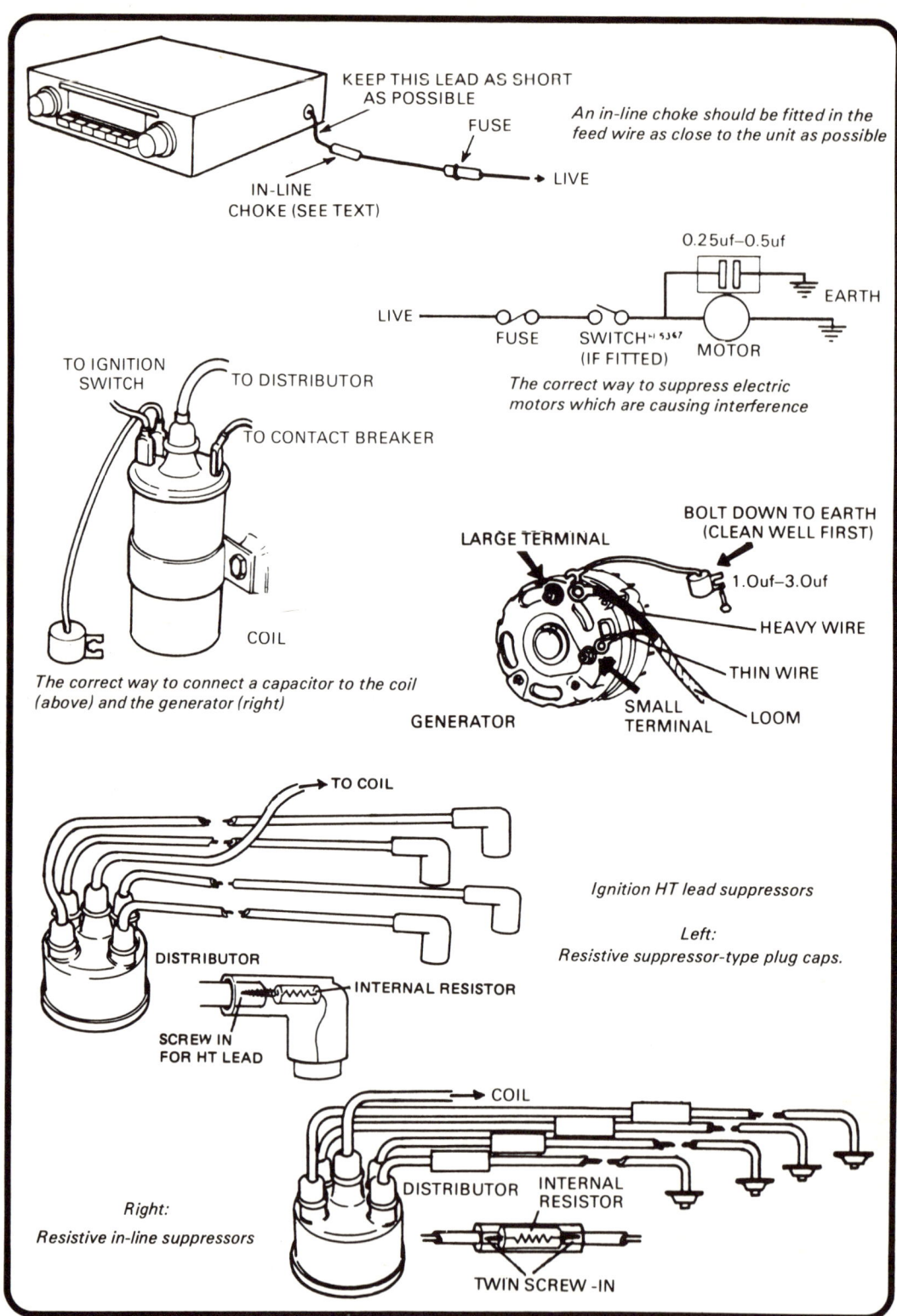

KEEP THIS LEAD AS SHORT AS POSSIBLE

FUSE

An in-line choke should be fitted in the feed wire as close to the unit as possible

IN-LINE CHOKE (SEE TEXT)

LIVE

0.25uf–0.5uf

LIVE

FUSE

SWITCH (IF FITTED)

MOTOR

EARTH

The correct way to suppress electric motors which are causing interference

TO IGNITION SWITCH

TO DISTRIBUTOR

TO CONTACT BREAKER

COIL

The correct way to connect a capacitor to the coil (above) and the generator (right)

LARGE TERMINAL

BOLT DOWN TO EARTH (CLEAN WELL FIRST)

1.0uf–3.0uf

HEAVY WIRE

THIN WIRE

LOOM

SMALL TERMINAL

GENERATOR

TO COIL

DISTRIBUTOR

INTERNAL RESISTOR

SCREW IN FOR HT LEAD

Ignition HT lead suppressors

Left:
Resistive suppressor-type plug caps.

COIL

DISTRIBUTOR

INTERNAL RESISTOR

TWIN SCREW -IN

Right:
Resistive in-line suppressors

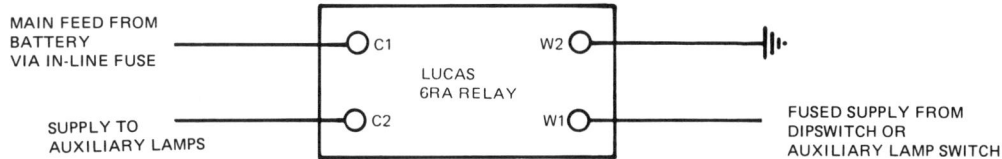

Typical connections for auxiliary lamps using a relay

Radios and tape players

A radio or tape player is an expensive item to buy, and will only give its best performance if fitted properly. It's useless to expect concert hall performance from a unit that's suspended from the dash panel by string with its speaker resting on the back seat or parcel shelf! If you don't wish to do the installation yourself there are many in-car entertainment specialists who can do the fitting for you.

Make sure that the unit purchased is of the same polarity as the car, or that units with adjustable polarity are correctly set before commencing installation. It's difficult to give specific information with regard to fitting, as final positioning of the radio/tape player, speakers and aerial is entirely a matter of personal preference. However the following paragraphs give guidelines to follow, which are relevant to all installations.

Radios

Most radios are a standardised size of 7 inches wide, by 2 inches deep – this ensures that they'll fit into the radio aperture provided in many cars. The following points should be borne in mind before deciding exactly where to fit the unit:

(a) *The unit must be in easy reach of the driver wearing a seat belt*

(b) *The unit must not be mounted close to an electric tachometer, the ignition switch and its wiring, or the flasher unit and associated wiring*

(c) *The unit must be mounted within reach of the aerial lead, and in such a place that the aerial lead will not have to be routed near the components detailed in paragraph (b)*

(d) *The unit should not be positioned in a place where it might cause injury to the car occupants in an accident for instance, under the dash panel above the driver's or passenger's legs*

(e) *The unit must be fitted really securely*

Aerials

The type of aerial used, and where you're going to fit it, is a matter of personal preference. In general, the taller the aerial, the better reception but there are limits to what is practicable. If you can, fit a fully retractable type – it saves an awful lot of problems with vandals and car-wash equipment. When choosing a suitable spot for the aerial, remember the following points:

(a) *The aerial lead should be as short as possible*

(b) *The aerial should be mounted as far away from the distributor and HT leads as possible*

(c) *The part of the aerial which protrudes beneath the mounting point must not foul the roadwheels, or anything else*

(d) *If possible the aerial should be positioned so that the coaxial lead does not have to be routed through the engine compartment*

(e) *The aerial should be mounted at a more-or-less vertical angle*

Tape players

Fitting instructions for both cartridge and cassette stereo tape players are the same, and in general the same rules apply as when fitting a radio. Tape players are not usually prone to electrical interference like radios – although it can occur – so positioning is not so critical. If possible the player should be mounted on an even keel. Also it must be possible for a driver wearing a seat belt to reach the unit in order to change, or turn over, tapes.

Radio interference suppression

Books have been written on the subject, so we're not going to be able to tell you a lot in this small space. To reduce the possibility of your radio picking up unwanted interference, an in-line choke should be fitted in the feed wire and the set itself must be earthed really securely. The next step is to start connecting capacitors to reduce the amount of interference being generated by the different circuits of the car's electrics. The accompanying illustrations show the various interference generators and give **83** capacitor values for the suppressors. When it comes to the ignition HT leads, these are resistors which can either be suppressor-type plug caps or in-line suppressors; if you're already using resistive HT leads (those with the carbon filling), they're already doing the job for you.

Visibility aids

Wing and door mirros

Recent EEC legislation has done wonders for the looks of exterior mirrors. In addition to being functional, they must now have no projections to catch clothing or other cars, and must fold flat when struck. The result is a new wave of products in all shapes and sizes, some of which can be sprayed to match up with the existing car finish. There's also been a marked swing recently from wing mirrors to the door-mounted kind, fitted as standard to some models.

Choose mirrors which you think will suit the car's styling and, having got them, select the mounting point carefully. You'll get a good idea of where the best place is by simply looking at other cars, but get someone to hold the mirror while you sit in the driving seat just to make sure you can see all you need to.

When fitting mirrors you'll first need to mark the hole position; then do likewise for the other side. Some door mirrors have a bolt type fixing, which will mean removing the door trim panel; others are simply attached by self-tapping screws. For the larger holes, check the size needed and, if you can, select a drill this size plus, where applicable, a smaller one to make a pilot hole. If you haven't got a large enough drill, you'll have to drill one or more smaller holes and file out to the correct size. Don't forget to remove any burrs from the hole afterwards, then apply a little primer to cover the bare metal edges. When the primer's dry you can fit the mirror following the makers' instructions, then swivel it to get the best rear view.

For mirrors which only need self-tapping screws, make sure the drill used for the holes isn't too big. Ideally it should be fractionally larger than the thread root diameter – it's better to make sure that the hole's on the small side and enlarge it if necessary, rather than start off with a hole that's too big for the screws to bite properly.

Rear window demisters

At one time, if your car wasn't fitted with a heated rear window as standard equipment, about the only remedy was a stick-on clear panel designed to act a bit like double glazing. They didn't usually work very well and frequently came unstuck too. Now they've been more or less superseded by the element type of stick-on demister. These act more like the genuine article, consisting of a metal foil element which is peeled off a backing sheet and stuck on the inside surface of the rear window glass. It has to be

MAG 'European' door mirror

wired up to the electrical system, of course, via a suitable fuse and switch, using sufficiently heavy cable and preferably incorporating a warning lamp as it will take quite a large current and shouldn't be left on inadvertently. The great thing about these devices is that they do work, and are very moderately priced.

Headlamp conversions

Still on the subject of better visibility, if your problem's seeing in the dark then you might well consider uprating your headlamps instead of eating all those carrots! A number of conversions are available, and mostly they're fitted by simply interchanging with the old light units, no wiring modifications being needed (see *In an Emergency* for headlight removals).

Comfort

Sound reducing kits

Longer journeys can be more pleasant if your car's comfortable to drive, and a couple of suggestions on this theme may be welcome.

Very few cars have yet been produced in which the noise level, particularly at motorway speeds, is all that could be desired. For economy reasons, most manufacturers put only a certain amount of underfelt and sound-deadening material into their cars, and a further improvement can usually be made by fitting one of the proprietary kits. These are usually tailored to fit individual models, and consist of sections of felt-like material which are glued in place under carpets, inside hollow sections, boot lid, etc., in accordance with instructions. The material can also be bought in rolls for DIY cutting, using the carpets etc as templates.

Seats

If your seats are showing signs of old age (and new covers won't disguise the sagging, when you sit in them) then you can of course have them rebuilt by an upholstery specialist. On the other hand, if you feel that the seats in the Cavalier aren't quite to your liking, you could think about replacing at least the driver's seat by one of the special bucket-types available. To look at these you'll need to find an accessory shop stocking the more motor sport orientated goods.

Miscellaneous

Electronic ignition

Such systems are many and varied and most are widely advertised. The makers claim easier starting, better performance and lower fuel consumption as the main advantages, and on the whole these claims

are substantiated in practice. However, before buying one of these kits we suggest you stop and consider whether your mileage and type of driving make the expenditure worthwhile. Get other advice, preferably from someone who's fitted such a system to his own car. Consider, too, whether you're capable of installing it yourself, otherwise you'll have to pay for fitting as well.

There are several types of electronic ignition — some retain the conventional contact-breaker in the car's distributor while others replace this by a magnetic triggering device. Even where the contact points are retained they're no longer likely to burn and therefore shouldn't need renewing very frequently — but this doesn't in itself amount to much of a saving.

Roof racks

Many an owner has to resort to a roof rack from time to time, even if it's only for family holidays. The types available are very varied, but they normally rely on clips attached to the water drain channel above the doors. If you're buying, select a size that suits your requirements (make sure that it's not too wide for the roof!) and don't overload it.

When fitting the roof rack, position it squarely on the roof, preferably towards the front rather than the rear. After it's loaded, by the way, recheck the tension of the attachment bracket screws. Don't keep the roof rack on when it's not wanted; it offers too much wind resistance and creates a surprising amount of noise (see *Save It!*).

Wide wheels

With increasing petrol and insurance costs, and decreasing speed limits, many motorists have stopped trying to get the ultimate in performance from a given engine size and drifted towards other things. One of these things, which not only smartens up the car but can also improve roadholding considerably, is a set of wide wheels.

You can get steel wide wheels which are less than half the price of a new radial tyre, but most people prefer the look of the light alloy ones. Practically all popular types are made from LM25 aluminium alloy; prices vary, but they'll certainly cost you more than the tyre that goes with them. For anyone who really wants to spend some money (and there can't really be any justification for it for normal road use) there are the magnesium alloy types; these'll set you back about twice as much as the aluminium alloy ones. You can even get steel wire-spoked wheels if you want your Cavalier to look really sporty.

There was a time when all light alloy wheels had a bad reputation, but this seems to have improved considerably with the more modern casting **85** techniques. They can still be porous, which could mean that you'll need a tube with the tyre if you're going to keep the air in, but they're normally sealed during manufacture to help overcome this. The wheels need to be treated with a little more care than steel wheels. To prevent corrosion setting in, it's important to keep them clean, particularly if there's salt on the roads, and to relacquer them from time to time. Don't drive into kerbs; a steel wheel might only suffer a dented rim but you can easily knock a piece out of a light alloy rim and that's the end of it.

When you're having tyres fitted, extra care must be taken to prevent the rim being damaged, and it won't do any harm to remind the tyre fitter at the time. Any balancing weights must be the stick-on type, not the ordinary clip-round-the-rim kind. The tyres themselves must be suitable for the rims, and because there are so many types around you'll have to take some advice from the wheel and tyre supplier.

One last point — flashy wheels are worth something on the thieves' market too, so it's worthwhile investing in lockable wheel nuts if your car's likely to be left unattended in lonely car parks for any length of time.

Steering wheels

One of the most popular, easily fitted accessories is a special steering wheel. Many types are available but it's also necessary to buy a boss which fits on to the steering column shaft, to which the steering wheel is then attached. No problems should be encountered when fitting a steering wheel or boss, once the old steering wheel has been taken off.

First prise out the medallion located in the centre of the steering wheel. Make sure the front wheels are in the straight-ahead position, then unscrew the steering wheel retaining nut with a a suitable box or socket spanner. Carefully pull the steering wheel off the shaft — if it's tight you'll have to use a puller. **Don't** attempt to jar the wheel off or you'll damage the collapsible steering column.

When you've finally, after much cursing, removed the original steering wheel you can commence to fit the new one. It's always better, if possible, to bolt the new steering wheel to the boss before attempting to slide the boss on to the steering column spines. When you're satisfied that the steering wheel spokes are lying evenly and the roadwheels are pointing straight ahead you can tighten the steering wheel nut.

Mudflaps

You're probably aware that both front and rear wheel arches can be fitted with mudflaps. These will not only protect your car's underside and paintwork from flying stones, but will also earn the thanks of following drivers owing to the reduction in spray during wet weather. Fitting's straightforward and is usually by means of clamping brackets and screws.

Specialist fitments

We've now covered most of the main items likely to interest the average owner from the DIY fitting angle. Such things as towbars and sunshine or vinyl roofs, while practical or desirable, are beyond the scope both of this book and of the ordinary car owner. We therefore recommend that for any major accessory of this kind you consult the appropriate specialist who'll be able to give an estimate of the cost, as well as carrying out the work properly and safely.

Troubleshooting

We've gone to great lengths in this book to provide as much information on your car as we think necessary for satisfactory running and servicing. Hopefully, you won't need to use this Section but there's always a possibility (rather than a probability!) that something will go wrong, and by reference to the charts that follow you should be able to pinpoint the trouble even if you can't actually fix it yourself.

The charts are broken down into the main systems of the car, and where there's a fairly straightforward remedy — the sort you can tackle yourself — bold type is used to highlight it. Further information on that particular item will normally be found elsewhere in the book; look up the particular component or system in the index to find the correct page. In some cases a reference number will be found (eg T1/1); by looking up this number in the accompanying cross-reference table, you'll find more information on that particular fault.

When confronted with a fault, try to think calmly and logically about the symptom(s) of the car concerned and you, soon be able to work out what the fault *can't* be. Check or substitute one item at a time, otherwise when you do clear the fault you may not know exactly what was causing it. The commonest cause of difficulty in starting, especially in winter, is a poor spark at the plugs combined with a slow cranking speed from the starter motor. Make sure that your battery's kept fully charged and that the HT leads and coil and distributor caps aren't covered in condensation, and you should save yourself some trouble. **87**

TROUBLESHOOTER 1:

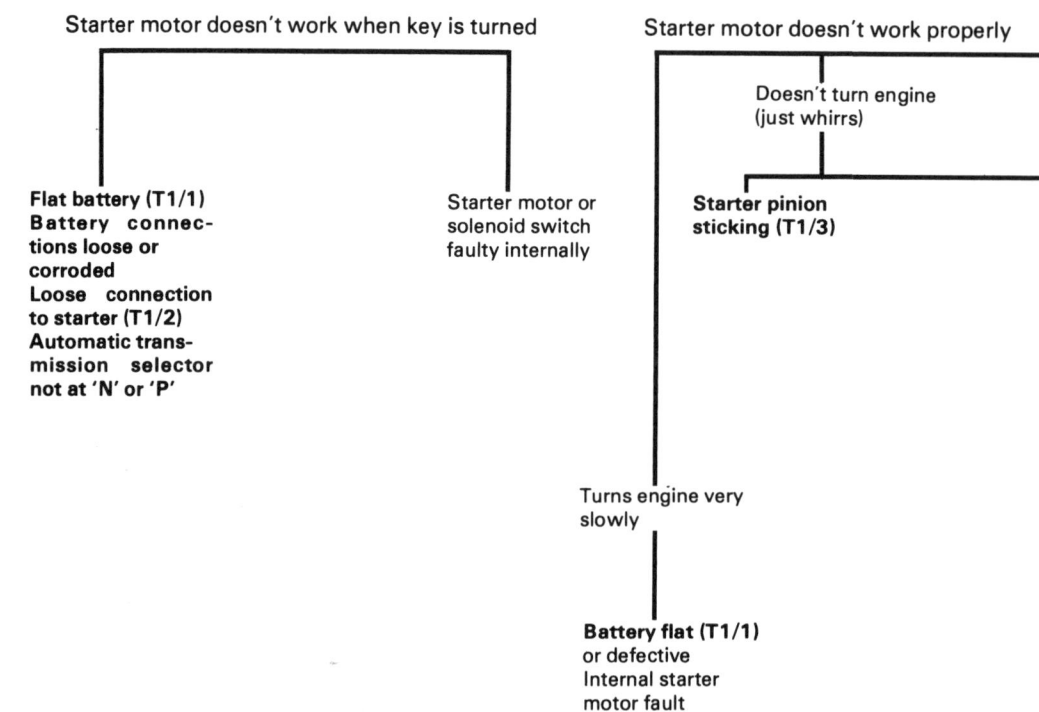

Starter motor doesn't work when key is turned

Flat battery (T1/1)
Battery connec-
tions loose or
corroded
Loose connection
to starter (T1/2)
Automatic trans-
mission selector
not at 'N' or 'P'

Starter motor or
solenoid switch
faulty internally

Starter motor doesn't work properly

Doesn't turn engine
(just whirrs)

Starter pinion
sticking (T1/3)

Turns engine very
slowly

Battery flat (T1/1)
or defective
Internal starter
motor fault

ENGINE – STARTING

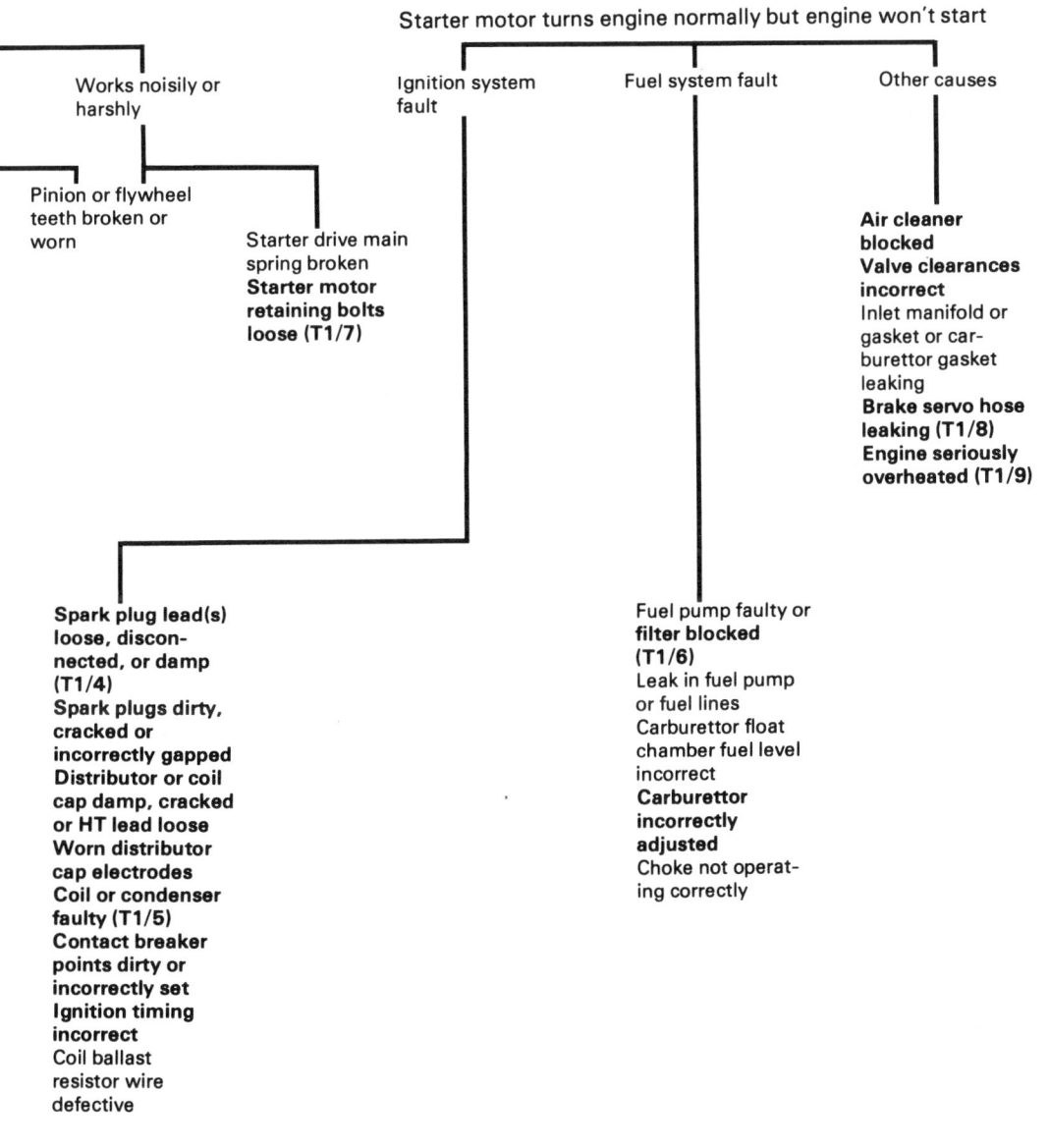

Starter motor turns engine normally but engine won't start

Works noisily or harshly

Ignition system fault

Fuel system fault

Other causes

Pinion or flywheel teeth broken or worn

Starter drive main spring broken
Starter motor retaining bolts loose (T1/7)

Air cleaner blocked
Valve clearances incorrect
Inlet manifold or gasket or car- burettor gasket leaking
Brake servo hose leaking (T1/8)
Engine seriously overheated (T1/9)

Spark plug lead(s) loose, discon- nected, or damp (T1/4)
Spark plugs dirty, cracked or incorrectly gapped
Distributor or coil cap damp, cracked or HT lead loose
Worn distributor cap electrodes
Coil or condenser faulty (T1/5)
Contact breaker points dirty or incorrectly set
Ignition timing incorrect
Coil ballast resistor wire defective

Fuel pump faulty or **filter blocked (T1/6)**
Leak in fuel pump or fuel lines
Carburettor float chamber fuel level incorrect
Carburettor incorrectly adjusted
Choke not operat- ing correctly

TROUBLESHOOTER 2:

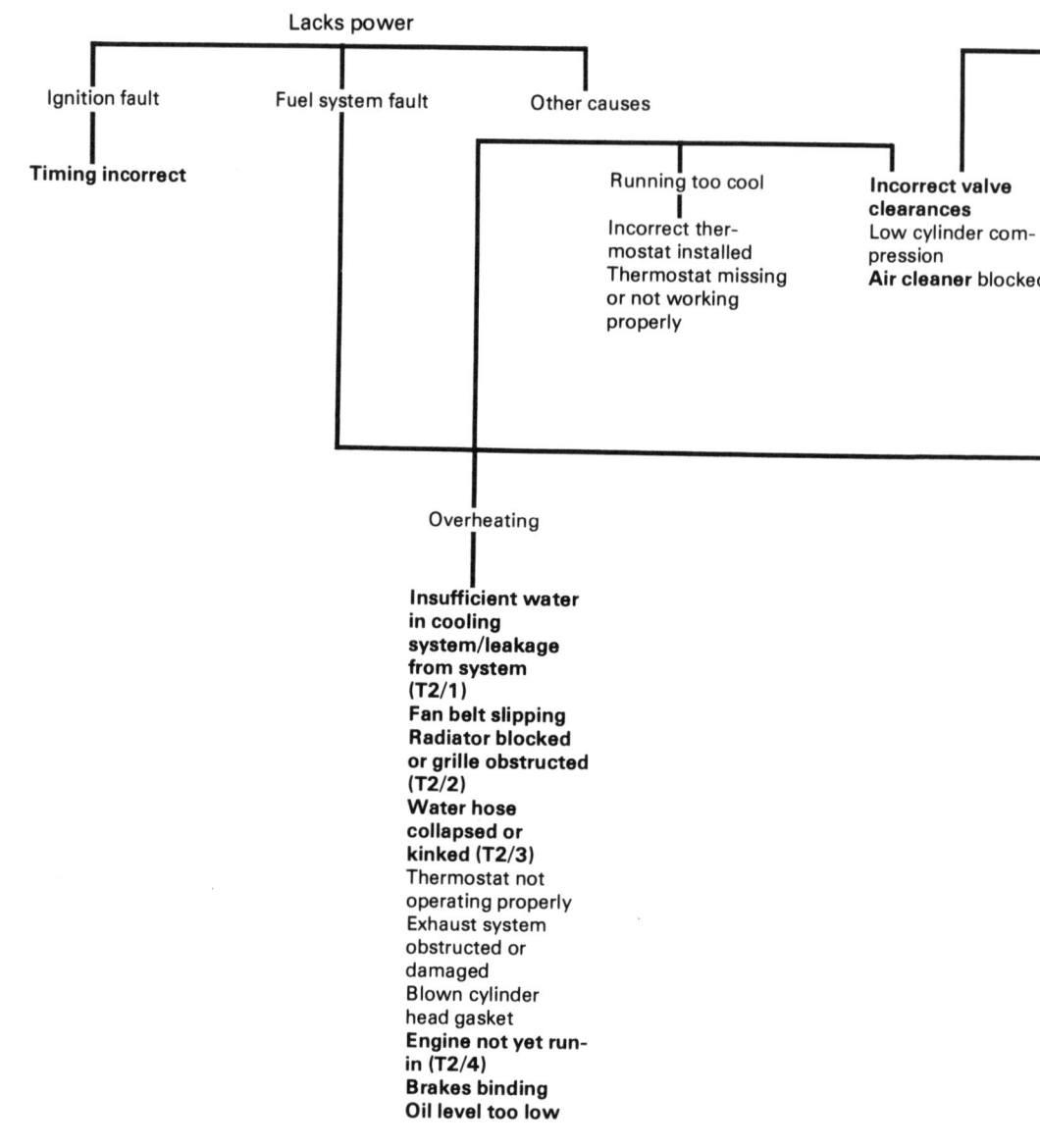

Lacks power

Ignition fault   Fuel system fault   Other causes

Timing incorrect

Running too cool

Incorrect ther-
mostat installed
Thermostat missing
or not working
properly

**Incorrect valve
clearances**
Low cylinder com-
pression
Air cleaner blocked

Overheating

**Insufficient water
in cooling
system/leakage
from system
(T2/1)
Fan belt slipping
Radiator blocked
or grille obstructed
(T2/2)
Water hose
collapsed or
kinked (T2/3)**
Thermostat not
operating properly
Exhaust system
obstructed or
damaged
Blown cylinder
head gasket
**Engine not yet run-
in (T2/4)
Brakes binding
Oil level too low**

ENGINE – RUNNING

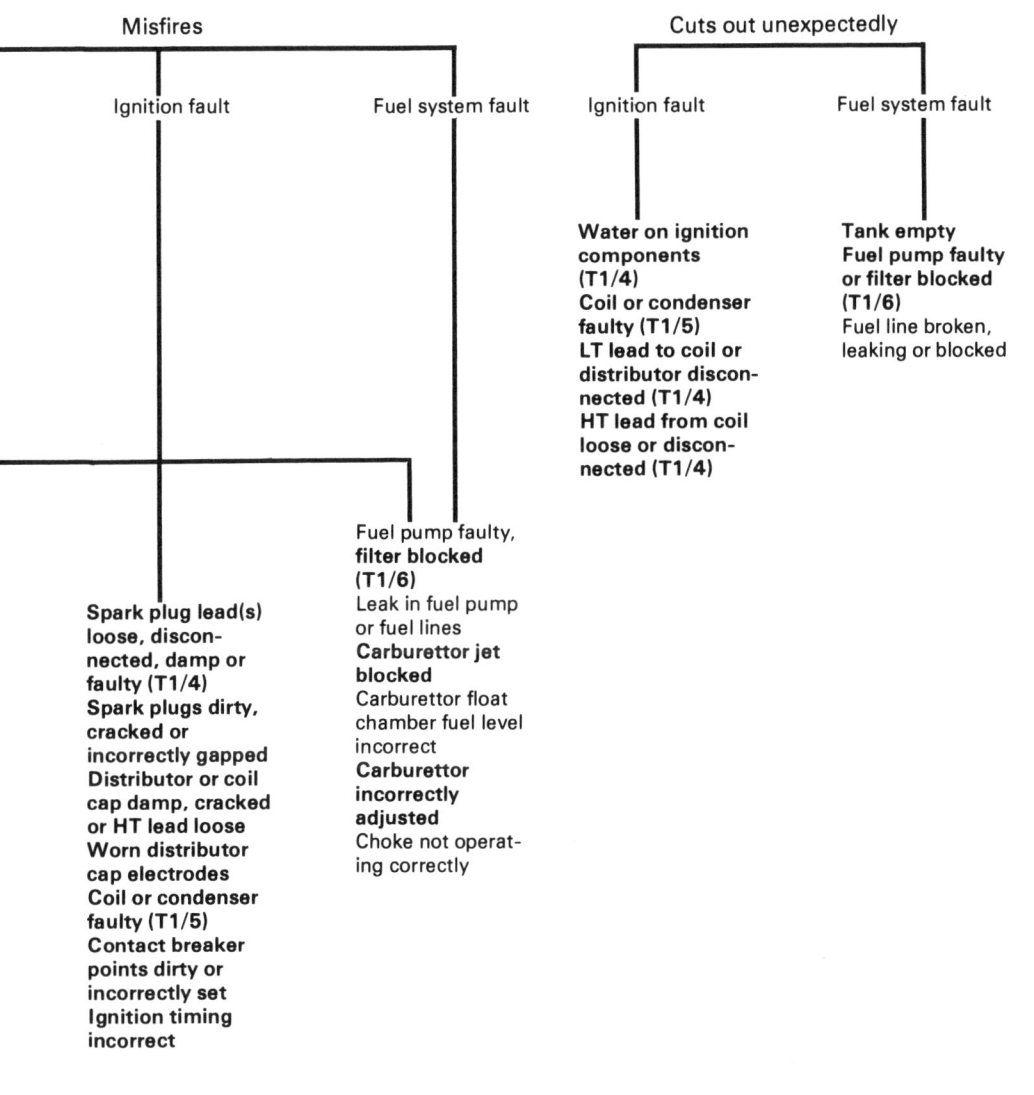

Misfires

Ignition fault

Fuel system fault

Cuts out unexpectedly

Ignition fault

Fuel system fault

**Water on ignition components (T1/4)
Coil or condenser faulty (T1/5)
LT lead to coil or distributor discon-nected (T1/4)
HT lead from coil loose or discon-nected (T1/4)**

**Tank empty
Fuel pump faulty or filter blocked (T1/6)**
Fuel line broken, leaking or blocked

Fuel pump faulty, **filter blocked (T1/6)**
Leak in fuel pump or fuel lines
Carburettor jet blocked
Carburettor float chamber fuel level incorrect
Carburettor incorrectly adjusted
Choke not operat-ing correctly

**Spark plug lead(s) loose, discon-nected, damp or faulty (T1/4)
Spark plugs dirty, cracked or incorrectly gapped
Distributor or coil cap damp, cracked or HT lead loose
Worn distributor cap electrodes
Coil or condenser faulty (T1/5)
Contact breaker points dirty or incorrectly set
Ignition timing incorrect**

TROUBLESHOOTER 3:

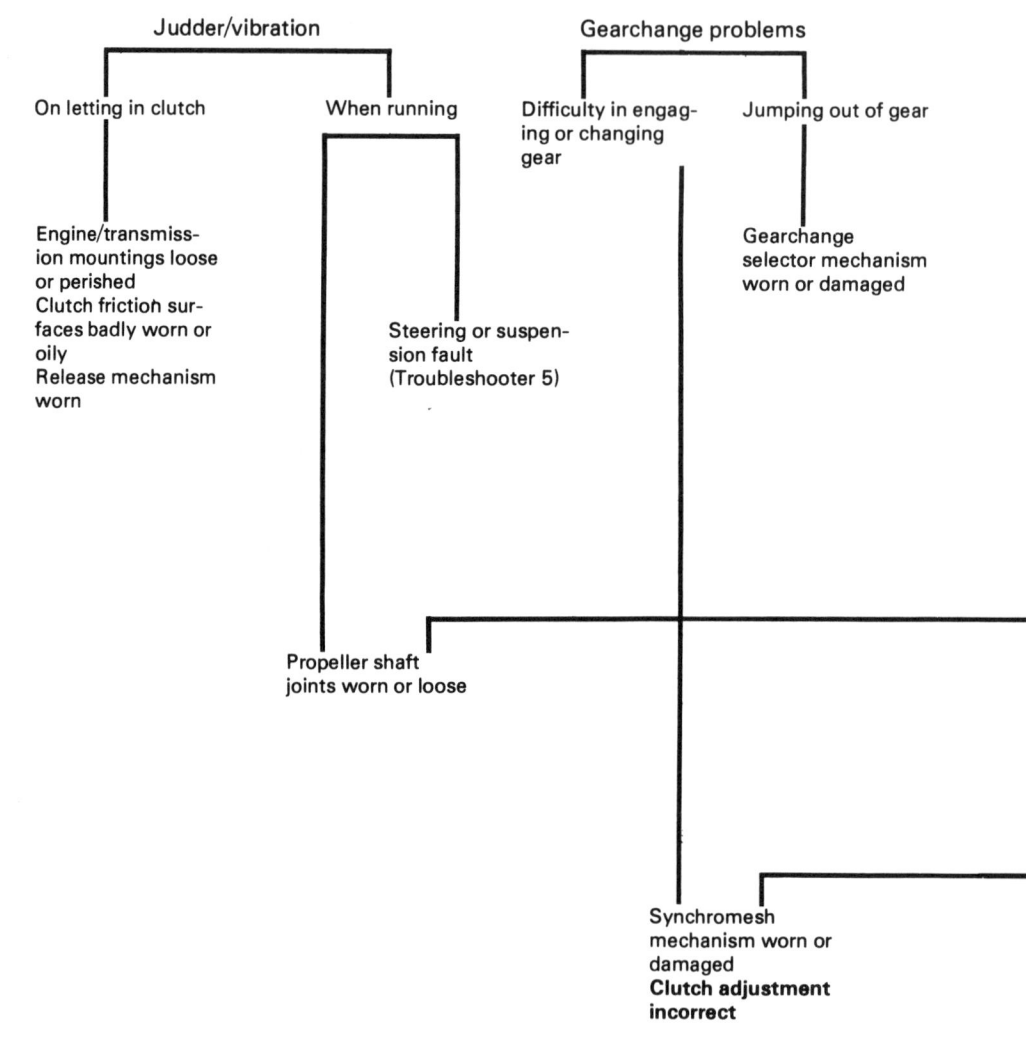

Judder/vibration

Gearchange problems

On letting in clutch

When running

Difficulty in engaging or changing gear

Jumping out of gear

Engine/transmission mountings loose or perished
Clutch friction surfaces badly worn or oily
Release mechanism worn

Steering or suspension fault
(Troubleshooter 5)

Gearchange selector mechanism worn or damaged

Propeller shaft joints worn or loose

Synchromesh mechanism worn or damaged
Clutch adjustment incorrect

CLUTCH & TRANSMISSION

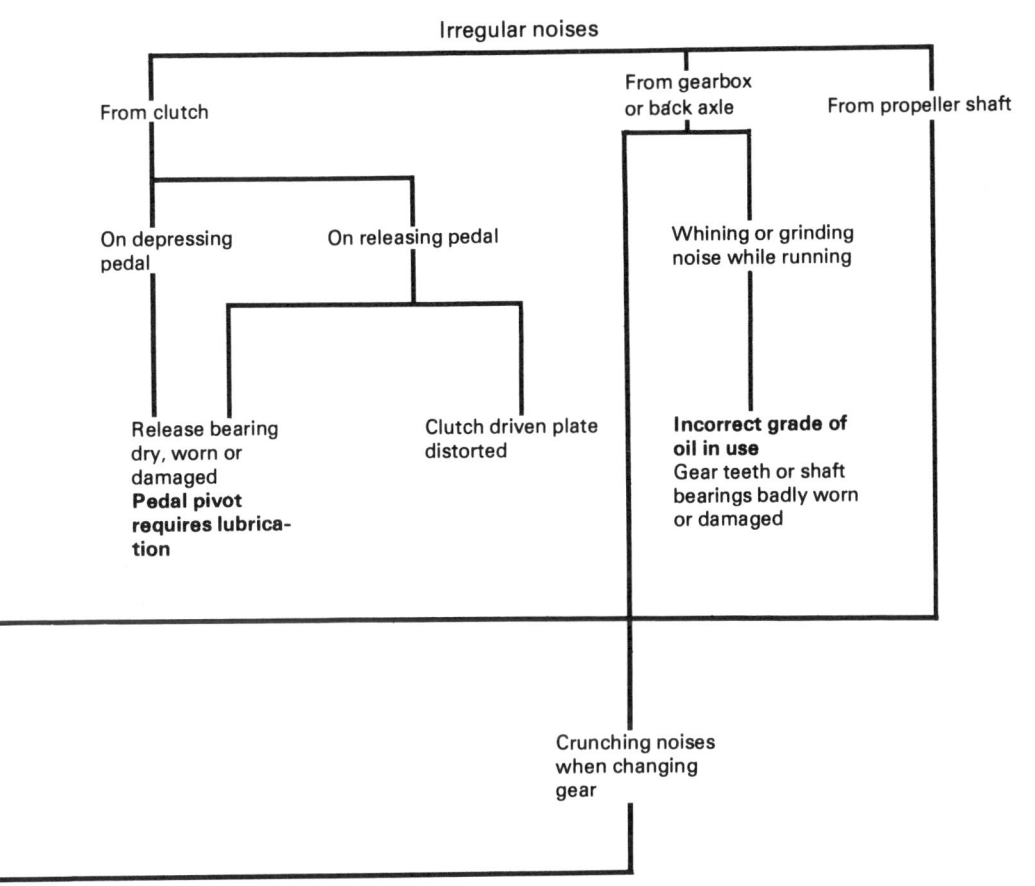

Irregular noises

From clutch

From gearbox or back axle

From propeller shaft

On depressing pedal

On releasing pedal

Whining or grinding noise while running

Release bearing dry, worn or damaged
Pedal pivot requires lubrication

Clutch driven plate distorted

Incorrect grade of oil in use
Gear teeth or shaft bearings badly worn or damaged

Crunching noises when changing gear

TROUBLESHOOTER 4:

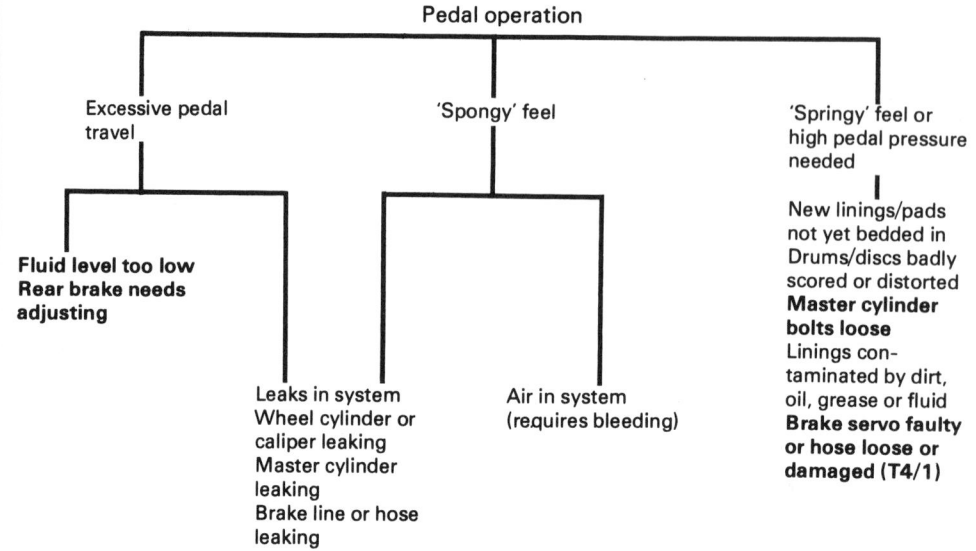

Pedal operation

Excessive pedal travel

**Fluid level too low
Rear brake needs adjusting**

Leaks in system
Wheel cylinder or caliper leaking
Master cylinder leaking
Brake line or hose leaking

'Spongy' feel

Air in system
(requires bleeding)

'Springy' feel or high pedal pressure needed

New linings/pads not yet bedded in
Drums/discs badly scored or distorted
Master cylinder bolts loose
Linings contaminated by dirt, oil, grease or fluid
Brake servo faulty or hose loose or damaged (T4/1)

TROUBLESHOOTER 5:

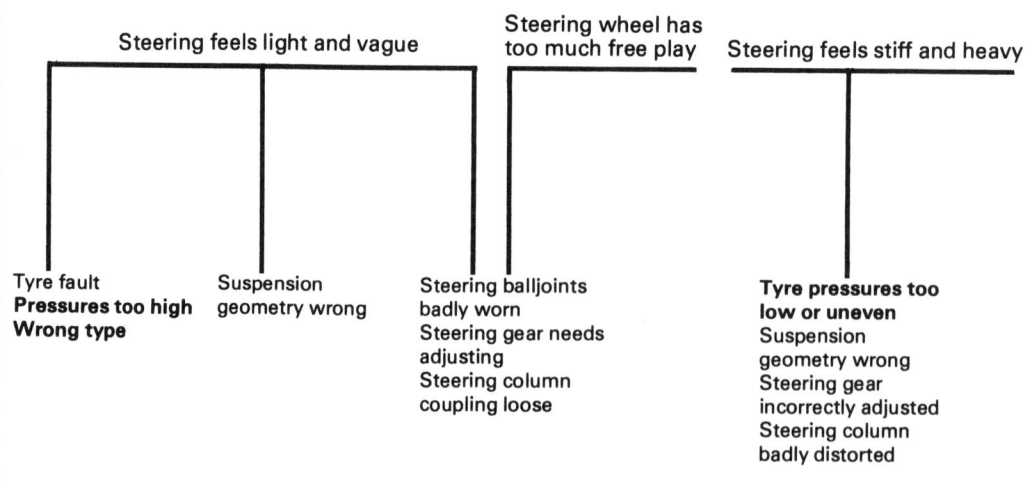

Steering feels light and vague

Steering wheel has too much free play

Steering feels stiff and heavy

Tyre fault
**Pressures too high
Wrong type**

Suspension geometry wrong

Steering balljoints badly worn
Steering gear needs adjusting
Steering column coupling loose

Tyre pressures too low or uneven
Suspension geometry wrong
Steering gear incorrectly adjusted
Steering column badly distorted

BRAKES

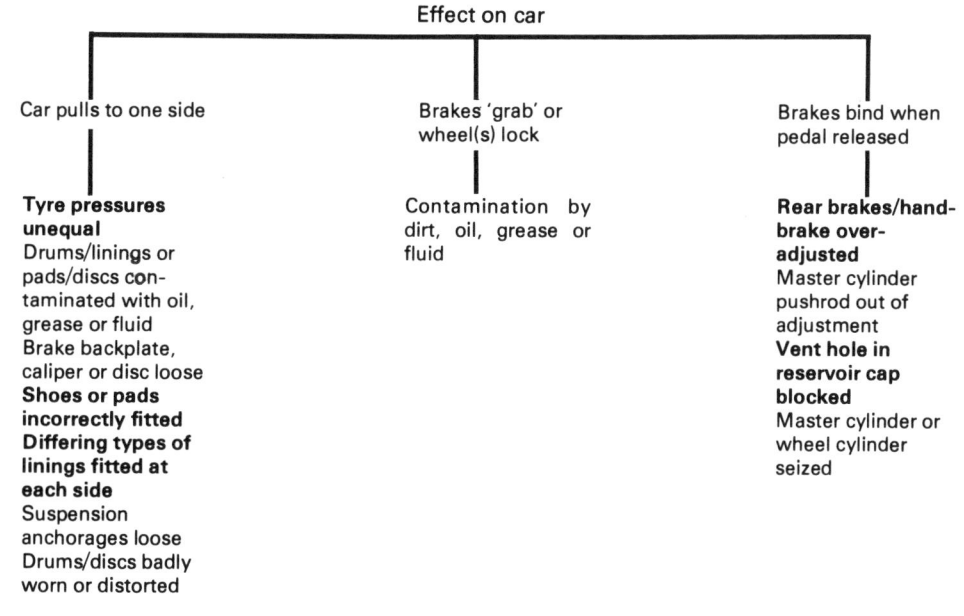

Effect on car

Car pulls to one side

Tyre pressures unequal
Drums/linings or pads/discs contaminated with oil, grease or fluid
Brake backplate, caliper or disc loose
Shoes or pads incorrectly fitted
Differing types of linings fitted at each side
Suspension anchorages loose
Drums/discs badly worn or distorted

Brakes 'grab' or wheel(s) lock

Contamination by dirt, oil, grease or fluid

Brakes bind when pedal released

Rear brakes/handbrake over-adjusted
Master cylinder pushrod out of adjustment
Vent hole in reservoir cap blocked
Master cylinder or wheel cylinder seized

STEERING/SUSPENSION

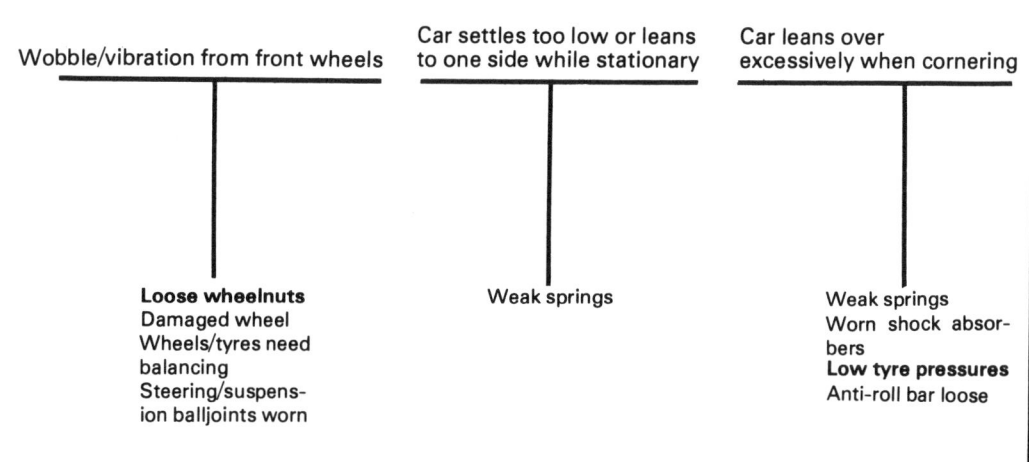

Wobble/vibration from front wheels

Loose wheelnuts
Damaged wheel
Wheels/tyres need balancing
Steering/suspension balljoints worn

Car settles too low or leans to one side while stationary

Weak springs

Car leans over excessively when cornering

Weak springs
Worn shock absorbers
Low tyre pressures
Anti-roll bar loose

TROUBLESHOOTER 6:

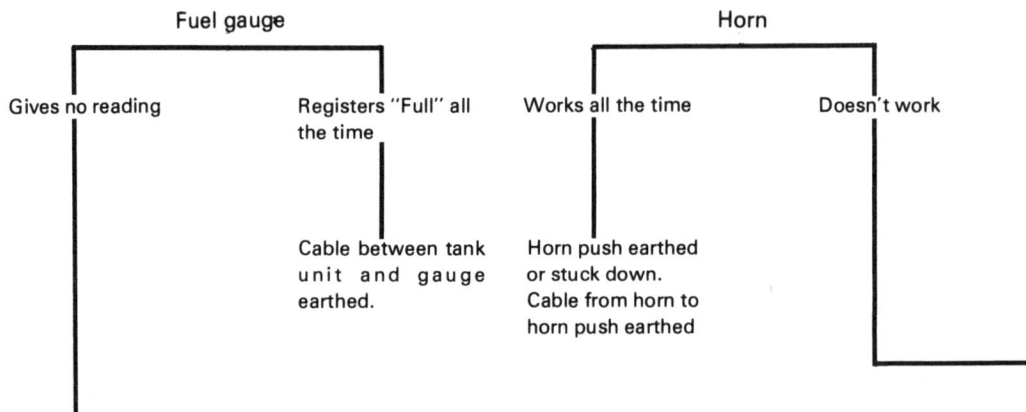

Fuel gauge

Horn

Gives no reading

Registers "Full" all
the time

Works all the time

Doesn't work

Cable between tank
unit and gauge
earthed.

Horn push earthed
or stuck down.
Cable from horn to
horn push earthed

Cable between tank
unit and gauge
broken or discon-
nected

NOTE: This chart assumes that the battery installed in your car is in good condition
and is of the correct specification, and that the terminal connections are clean and
tight. A car used frequently for stop-start motoring or for short journeys (particularly
in winter when lights, heater blower etc are likely to be in use) may need its battery
recharged at intervals to keep it serviceable. If an electrical problem occurs, don't
immediately suspect the starter or any other component without first checking that
the battery is capable of supplying its demands!

ELECTRICS

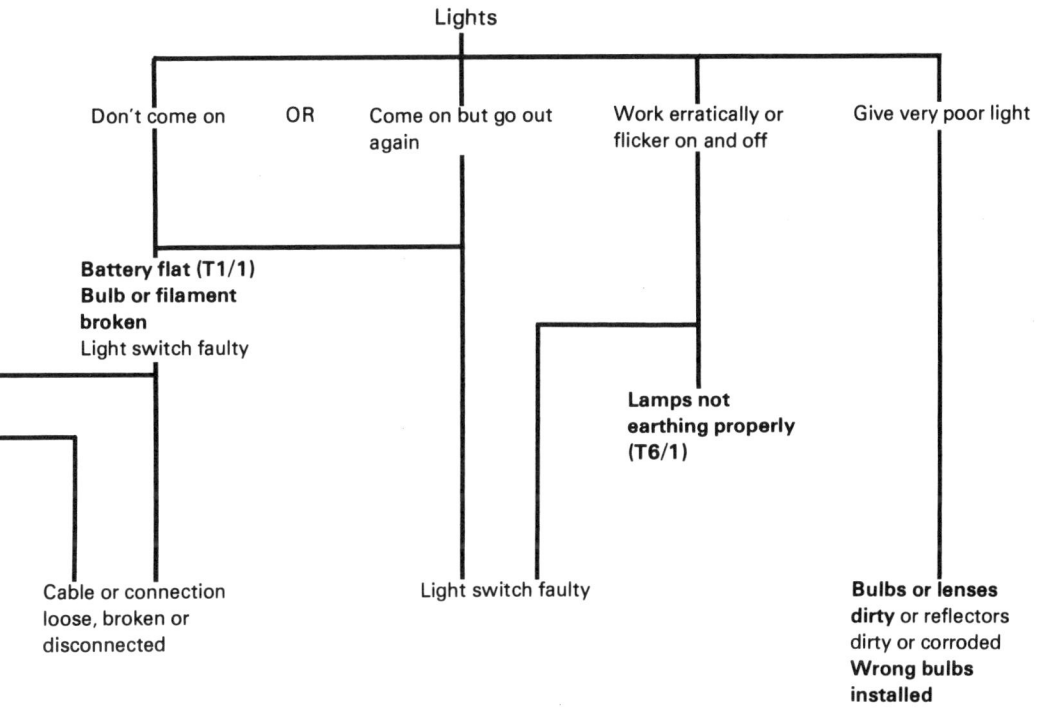

Lights

Don't come on   OR   Come on but go out again   Work erratically or flicker on and off   Give very poor light

Battery flat (T1/1)
Bulb or filament broken
Light switch faulty

Cable or connection loose, broken or disconnected

Light switch faulty

Lamps not earthing properly (T6/1)

Bulbs or lenses dirty or reflectors dirty or corroded
Wrong bulbs installed

A fault occurring in any other electrical equipment or accessory not specifically referred to can usually be traced to one of three main causes, ie blown fuse; loose or broken connection to power supply or earth; or internal fault in the component concerned.

CROSS-REFERENCE TABLE

TROUBLESHOOTER REFERENCE	ADDITIONAL INFORMATION
T1/1	Either charge the battery from a battery charger, or use jumper leads to start the car from another battery; make sure that the lead polarities are correct in both cases or you may do permanent damage, particularly if your car has an alternator.
T1/2	If the lead's loose, disconnect the battery earth lead then tighten the connection on the starter motor. Reconnect the battery earth lead.
T1/3	If the starter pinion's jammed in mesh with the flywheel teeth, try engaging top gear and rocking the car to-and-fro to free it.
T1/4	Make sure all the connections are tight, then wipe the leads clean and dry with a lint-free cloth. Use an ignition system waterproofer (eg WD40 or Damp Start) to prevent problems in the future.
T1/5	An ignition coil or condenser is a simple item to fit, but make a note of the connections before removing them, and ensure that the replacement coil is the correct type. Renewal of the condenser is covered in the 24 000 mile Service Schedule.
T1/6	To check the operation of the pump, detach the fuel outlet pipe (that's the one that goes to the carburettor) and turn the engine briefly on the starter motor. Take care you don't spill fuel on the hot exhaust! Cleaning the fuel pump filter is covered in the 12 000 mile Service Schedule.
T1/7	It's easy enough to tighten the attachment bolts if you've got a box or socket spanner of the right size, but you'll need to hold it to prevent them turning.

TROUBLESHOOTER REFERENCE	ADDITIONAL INFORMATION
T1/8	For a temporary repair a leaking water hose can normally be bound up with adhesive tape or, better still, with a hose bandage available for this purpose.
T1/9	Wait till the system's cooled down, then top it up. If it happens a second time, get it looked at straight away or you could ruin your engine (if it hasn't happened already). If it's just a leaking water hose you can probably bind it up as in T1/8 (above) to get yourself home.
T2/1	See T1/9.
T2/2	Driving carefully will probably get you home. An air line on the radiator core will clean out the dirt that's accumulated; if it's blocked internally, use a proprietary flushing compound (24 000 mile Service Schedule).
T2/3	You may be able to repair the hose temporarily, as in T1/8, but it'll almost certainly mean a new one as soon as possible.
T2/4	Drive more slowly!
T4/1	Provided there's no loss of hydraulic fluid, you'll need a little extra pedal effort for braking but that's all. It may be possible to temporarily repair the vacuum hose as in T1/8.
T6/1	Remove the lamp lenses (see *In an Emergency*) and check for signs of rust. Where there's rust, scrape it off and apply a little Vaseline.

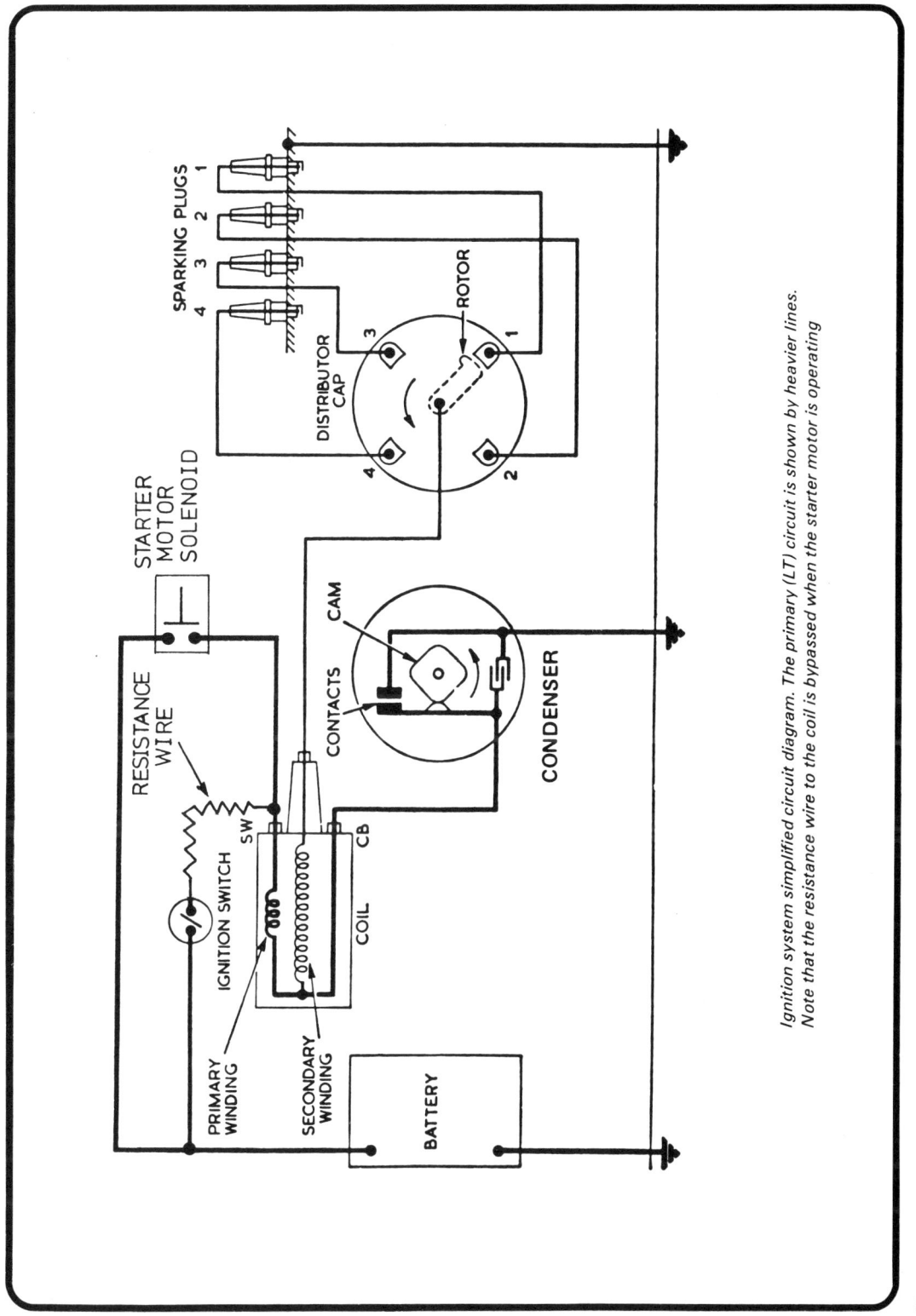

Ignition system simplified circuit diagram. The primary (LT) circuit is shown by heavier lines.
Note that the resistance wire to the coil is bypassed when the starter motor is operating

CAR JARGON EXPLAINED

We hope there isn't much in this Handbook that you can't understand. However, most of us – particularly if we're trying to learn more about an unfamiliar subject – will sooner or later come across the odd word or phrase that needs explaining. This alphabetical list should help you understand the language spoken by your garage man, 'expert' neighbour, or that inevitable chap in the local...

A

Accelerator pump: A device attached to many *carburettors* which adds a spurt of extra fuel to the carburettor mixture when the accelerator pedal is suddenly pressed down.

Additives: Compounds which are added to petrol and lubricating oil to improve their quality and performance.

Advance and retard: A system for altering the ignition timing – the time in the firing cycle at which the ignition spark occurs. The spark timing is normally a few degrees of *crankshaft* revolution before the *piston* reaches the top of its stroke, and is expressed as so many degrees before top-dead-centre (BTDC). It's altered by devices in the *distributor* which detect changes in engine speed and load. Broadly speaking, as the engine speeds up the ignition is advanced (greater angle BTDC) but if there is a heavy engine load the ignition is retarded (smaller angle BTDC).

AF: An abbreviation of 'across flats', the way in which many nuts, bolt heads and spanners are now identified. It's preceded by an Imperial or metric unit of measurement – e.g. $\frac{1}{2}$ in AF or 11 mm AF.

Air cooling: Alternative method of engine cooling in which no water is used. An engine-driven fan forces air at high velocity over the engine surfaces, which are enclosed by cowling. Normally an *oil cooler* is incorporated in the air flow to assist the rate of heat loss.

Alternator: A device for converting rotating mechanical energy into electrical energy. In modern cars, it has superseded the *dynamo* for charging the battery because of its much greater efficiency.

Ammeter: A device for measuring the current supplied to the battery from the *dynamo* or *alternator,* or drawn from the battery by the car lights, wipers, radio etc.

Antifreeze: A chemical compound mixed with the cooling system water to lower the temperature at which the coolant freezes.

Anti-roll bar: A spring-steel bar mounted transversely across a car which counteracts the natural tendency for the car to lean over when cornering.

Aquaplaning: A phrase used to describe the action of a tyre skating across water.

Automatic transmission: A type of *gearbox* which selects the correct gear ratio automatically according to the engine speed and load.

B

Balljoint: A ball-and-socket type joint, used in steering and *suspension* systems, which permits relative movement in more than one plane.

Battery condition indicator: A voltmeter connected via the ignition switch to the car battery. Unlike an *ammeter* (which it's tending to supersede), it will warn you of impending battery failure.

Bearing: Metal or other hard wearing surface against which another part moves or rotates, and which is designed (and usually lubricated) to withstand the resulting friction.

Bendix drive: A device on many types of starter motor which allows the motor to be coupled to the *flywheel* for engine starting, then disengages when the engine commences to run.

BHP: See *Horsepower.*

Big end: The end of a *connecting rod* which is attached to the *crankshaft.* It incorporates a *bearing* and transmits the linear movement of the con-rod to the rotary motion of the crankshaft.

Bleed nipple (or valve): A hollow screw with a tapered seat which allows air or fluid to be bled out of a system when it is loosened.

Brake caliper: That part of a *disc brake* system which houses the *brake pads* and the *hydraulic* operating *pistons.*

Brake fade: A temporary loss of braking efficiency due to overheating of the brake friction material.

Brake pad: That part of a *disc brake* system which comprises the friction material and a metal backing plate.

Brake shoe: That part of a *drum brake* system which comprises the friction material and a curved metal former.

Breather: A device which allows fresh air into a system or allows contaminated air out.

Bucket tappet: A cup (or bucket) shaped piece of metal used in some engines to transmit the rotary *camshaft* movement to an up-and-down movement for *valve* operation.

Bump stop: A hard rubber device used in many *suspension* systems to prevent the moving parts from lifting the bodyframe during violent suspension movements.

C

Camber angle: The angle at which the front wheels are set from the vertical, when viewed from the front of the car. Positive camber is the amount in degrees by which the wheels are tilted outwards at the top.

Cam follower: A cylindrical piece of metal used to transmit the rotary *camshaft* movement to an up-and-down movement for *valve* operation.

Camshaft: A rotating shaft with lobes or cams used to operate the engine *valves*.

Carbon fibre leads: Black, string-like cores in the centre of some spark plug *HT* leads, which don't need separate radio and *TV* suppressors.

Carburettor: A device which is used to mix air and fuel in the correct proportions for all conditions of engine running. There are two main types: those with a number of fixed *jets*, and those with a single jet with a moving needle in it. In the former type, the different jets come into operation at different conditions of throttle opening, engine speed and engine load; in the latter type, the *needle jet* is controlled by a moving *piston*, the position of which depends on the amount of suction in the engine inlet *manifold.*

Castor angle: The angle between the front wheel pivot points and a vertical line when viewed from the side of the car. Positive castor is when the axis is inclined rearwards.

Centrifugal advance: System of ignition *advance and retard* incorporated in many *distributors* in which weights rotating on a shaft alter the ignition timing according to engine speed.

Choke: This has two common meanings. It is used to describe the device which shuts off some of the air in a *carburettor* during cold starting, and may be either manually or automatically operated. It's also used as a general term to describe the carburettor throttle bore.

Clutch: A friction device which allows two rotating devices to be coupled together smoothly, without the need for either rotating part to stop.

Coil spring: A spiral of spring steel used in many *suspension* systems.

Combustion chamber: Shaped area in the *cylinder head* into which the fuel/air mixture is compressed by the *piston* and in which combustion of the mixture is effected by the *spark plug.*

Compression ratio (CR): A term used to describe the amount by which the fuel/air mixture is compressed, and expressed as a number. For example, an 8.5 : 1 compression ratio means that the volume of fuel/air when the *piston* is at the bottom of its stroke is 8.5 times that when the piston is at the top of its stroke.

Compression tester: A special type of pressure gauge screwed into the *spark plug* hole which shows the *cylinder* compression when the engine is turning but not firing.

Condenser (capacitor): A device in the *distributor* which stores electrical energy and prevents excessive sparking at the *contact breaker* points.

Connecting rod (con-rod): Rod in the engine connecting the *piston* to the *crankshaft.*

Constant velocity (CV) joint: A joint used in *driveshafts,* where the speed of the input shaft is exactly the same as the speed of the output shaft at any angle of rotation. This does not occur in ordinary *universal joints.*

Contact breaker: The device in the *distributor* which comprises the electrical points (or contacts), and a cam which opens and closes them to operate the *HT* electrical circuit which provides the spark at the *spark plug.*

Crossflow cylinder head: A *cylinder head* in which the inlet and exhaust *valves* are on opposite sides.

Crossply tyre: A tyre whose construction is such that the weave of the fabric material layers is running diagonally in alternately opposite directions to a line around the circumference.

Cubic capacity: The total volume within the *cylinders* which is swept by the *pistons.*

Cylinder head: That part of the engine which contains the *valves* and associated operating gear.

D

Damper: See *shock* absorber.

Dashpot: An oil-filled *cylinder* and *piston* used as a damping device in SU and Zenith/Stromberg CD type *carburettors.*

Dead axle (beam axle): The simplest form of axle, comprising a horizontal member attached to the chassis-frame by springs. This is used for the rear axle on some front-wheel-drive cars.

Decarbonizing ('decoking'): Removal of all carbon deposits from the *combustion chambers* of an engine.

De Dion axle: A rear axle comprising a cranked tube attached to the wheel hubs, with a separately **101**

mounted *differential* gear and *driveshafts. Suspension* is normally through *coil springs* between the wheel hubs and chassis frame.

Diaphragm: A stationary flexible membrane used in items such as fuel pumps. The diaphragm spring used in *clutches* is somewhat similar but is made from spring steel.

Diesel engine: An engine which relies upon the heat generated when compressing air to ignite the fuel, and which therefore doesn't need a *spark plug.* Diesel engines have much higher *compression ratios* than petrol engines, normally in the region of 20: 1.

Differential: A system of gears (generally known as a crownwheel and pinion) which allows the *torque* from the *propeller shaft* to be applied to the driving wheels. The torque is divided proportionately between the driving wheels to permit one wheel to turn faster than the other if required, for example during cornering.

DIN: This stand for Deutsche Industrie Norm (roughly equivalent to the British Standards Institution) and lays down international standards for measuring output, performance, etc., of motor vehicles.

Disc brake: A braking system where a rotating disc is clamped between hydraulically operated friction pads.

Distributor: A collective term used to describe the *contact breaker, advance and retard* mechanisms, and associated parts of the *ignition system.*

Doughnut: A term used to describe the flexible rubber coupling used in some *driveshafts.*

Driveshaft: Name usually applied to the shaft (normally incorporating *universal* or *constant velocity joints*) which transmits the drive from a *transaxle* to one wheel; more commonly found in front-wheel-drive cars.

Drive train: A collective term used to describe the *gearbox, propeller shaft, final drive* and *half-shafts* of a front engine/rear wheel drive car.

Drum brake: A brake with friction linings on 'shoes', running inside a cylindrical drum attached to the wheel.

Dual circuit brakes: A *hydraulic* braking system comprising two separate fluid circuits, so that if one circuit becomes inoperative, braking power is still available from the other circuit at a reduced efficiency.

Dwell angle: The number of degrees of *distributor* cam rotation during which the *contact breaker* points are closed during the ignition cycle of one *cylinder.* The angle is altered by adjusting the points gap, and is a more accurate way of setting-up the *ignition system.*

Dynamo: A device for converting rotating mechanical energy into electrical energy. This is a heavier, less efficient. form of *generator* than the *alternator,* and has largely been superseded by it during recent years.

E

Earth strap: A flexible electrical connection between the battery and vehicle earth, or the engine/*gearbox* and chassis frame, to provide the return current-flow path in the electrical system.

Electrode: An electrical terminal or terminals, across which a spark occurs e.g., in a *spark plug* or *distributor* cap.

Electrolyte: A current-conducting solution of water and sulphuric acid, which is the liquid inside the car battery.

Electronic ignition: An *ignition system* incorporating electronic components which can produce a much greater spark voltage than in conventional systems.

Emission control: The prevention or reduction of the emission into the atmosphere of noxious fumes and gases from the engine and fuel tank of a motor vehicle. Required to varying degrees by the laws of different countries, it is effected by design and by special devices.

Epicyclic gears (planetary gears): A gear system used in many *automatic transmissions* where there is a centre 'sun' wheel around which smaller 'planet' gears inside a 'planet carrier' rotate.

Exhaust gas analyser: An instrument used for the measurement of pollutants (mainly carbon monoxide) in an exhaust system.

Expansion tank: A container used in many modern cooling systems to collect the overflow from the car's *radiator* as the coolant heats up and expands.

F

Filter: A device for extracting foreign particles from air or oil.

Final drive: A collective term (often expressed as a gearing ratio) for the crownwheel and pinion (see *Differential*).

Flat engine: Form of engine design in which the *cylinders* are positioned horizontally, usually with an equal number each side of a central *crankshaft.*

Float chamber: That part of a *carburettor* which contains a float and *needle valve* for controlling the fuel level.

Flywheel: A heavy rotating disc attached to the *crankshaft* used to smooth out the pulsating output from the *cylinders.*

Four stroke (cycle): A common term used to describe the four operating strokes of a *piston* in a conventional car engine. These are: (1) Induction —

drawing in the fuel/air mixture as the piston goes down; (2) Compression of the fuel/air mixture as the piston rises; (3) Power stroke where the piston is forced down after the fuel/air mixture has been ignited by the *spark plug* and (4) Exhaust stroke where the piston rises and pushes the burnt gases out of the *cylinder*. During these operations, the inlet and exhaust *valves* are opened and closed at the correct moment to allow the fuel/air mixture in, the exhaust gases out, or to provide a gas-tight compression chamber.

Fuel injection: A method of injecting fuel into an engine. Used in *Diesel* engines, and also on some petrol engines as a replacement for the *carburettor*.

G

Gasket: Compressible material used between two metal surfaces to make a leakproof joint.

Gearbox: A group of gears and shafts installed in a metal housing. Physically, this is positioned between the *clutch* and the *differential,* and is used to multiply the engine *torque*.

Generator: See *alternator* and *dynamo*.

H

Half-shaft: A rotating shaft, two of which are used to transmit the drive from the *differential* to the wheels.

Hardy-Spicer joint (Hooke's or Cardan joint): See *Universal joint*.

Helical gears: Gears in which the teeth are cut at a slant across the circumference to give smoother meshing and quieter running.

Horsepower: A measurement of the rate of doing work. Where brake horsepower *(BHP)* is referred to, it's the amount of work required to stop a moving body.

HT: Abbreviation of high tension (meaning high voltage). Used on connection with the ignition system.

Hydraulic: A term used to describe the operation of a system by means of fluid pressure.

I

Ignition system: The electrical system which provides the spark to ignite the air/fuel mixture in the engine. Normally it comprises the battery, ignition coil, *distributor, (contact breaker and condenser),* ignition switch, *spark plugs* and wiring.

Ignition timing: See *Advance and retard*.

Inertia reel: Automatic type of safety belt which permits the wearer to move freely in normal use but which locks to give restraint on sensing either sudden deceleration of the car or sudden movement of the wearer.

In-line engine: Engine in which the *cylinders* are positioned in one row as distinct from being e.g. a *flat* or *vee* formation.

J

Jet: A calibrated nozzle or orifice in a *carburettor* through which fuel is drawn for mixing with air.

Jump leads: Heavy electric cables fitted with clips to enable a vehicle's battery to be connected to an external one for emergency starting.

K

Kerb weight: The weight of a car, unladen but ready to be driven, i.e. with enough fuel, oil etc. to travel an arbitrary distance.

Kickdown: A device used on *automatic transmissions* which allows a lower gear to be selected by flooring the accelerator.

Kingpin: A device which allows the front wheels of a car to swivel.

L

Laminated windscreen: A windscreen which has a thin plastic layer sandwiched between two layers of toughened glass. Its advantage is that it doesn't shatter or craze over when hit.

Leading shoe: Brake shoe of which the leading end (the one moved by the operating *cylinder)* is reached first by a given point on the drum during normal forward rotation. A simple single-cylinder *drum brake* will have one leading and one trailing (the opposite) shoe.

Leaf spring: A spring commonly used on cars with a *live axle,* comprising several long steel plates clamped together.

Little end: The smaller end of the *connecting rod* which is attached to the *piston*.

Live axle: An axle through which power is transmitted to the rear wheels.

Loom: A complete vehicle wiring system, or section thereof (e.g. front loom) comprising all the necessary cables of predetermined colours and lengths to wire up the various circuits.

LT: Abbreviation of low tension (meaning low voltage). Used in connection with *ignition systems*. **103**

M

MacPherson strut: An independent front *suspension* system where the swivelling, springing and shock absorbing action of the wheel is dealt with by a single assembly.

Manifold: The device used for ducting the air/fuel mixture to the engine (inlet manifold), or the exhaust gases from the engine (exhaust manifold).

Master cylinder: A cylinder containing a *piston* and hydraulic fluid, directly coupled to a foot pedal (e.g. brake or clutch *master cylinder*). It's used for transmitting pressure to the brake or *clutch* operating mechanism.

Metallic paint: Paint finish incorporating minute particles of metal to give added lustre to the colour.

Multigrade: Lubricating oil whose *viscosity* covers that of several *monograde* oils, making it suitable for use over a wider range of operating conditions.

N

Needle bearing: Type of *bearing* in which needle or cone-shaped rollers are employed around the inner circumference, often used to reduce the space needed for the bearing.

Needle valve: A component of the *carburettor* which restricts the flow of fuel or fuel/air mixture according to its position relative to an orifice or *jet.*

Negative earth: Electrical system (now almost universally adopted) in which the negative terminal of the car battery is connected to the vehicle body, the polarity of all other electrical equipment being determined by this.

O

Octane rating: A scale rating introduced by the British Standards Institution for grading petrol.

OHC (overhead cam): Describes an engine in which the *camshaft* is situated above the *cylinder head,* and operates the *valve* gear directly without the need for *pushrods.*

OHV (Overhead valve): Describes an engine which has its *valves* in the *cylinder head* (as in *OHC*) but suggests that the valve gear is operated via *pushrods* from a *camshaft* situated lower in the engine. Practically all modern car engines are OHV but are not necessarily OHC.

Oil cooler: Small *radiator* fitted in the lubricating oil circuit and sited in a cooling airflow to dissipate heat from the oil. Used mainly in higher-performance engines.

104 **Overdrive**: A device coupled to a car *gearbox* which raises the output gear ratio above the normal 1 : 1 of top gear. Also used to describe a top gear ratio of greater than 1 : 1 found in some cars.

Oversteer: A tendency for a car to turn more tightly into a corner than intended.

P

PCV (Positive crankcase ventilation): A system which allows fumes and vapours which build up in the crankcase to be drawn into the engine for burning.

Pinion: A gear with a small number of teeth which meshes with one having a larger number of teeth.

Pinking: A metallic noise from the engine often caused by the *ignition timing* being too far advanced. The noise is the result of pressure waves which cause the cylinder walls to vibrate, when the ignited fuel/air is compressed.

Piston: Cylindrical component which slides in a closely-fitting metal tube or *cylinder* and transmits pressure. The pistons in an engine, for example, compress the fuel/air mixture, transmit the combustion power to the *crankshaft,* and exhaust the burnt gases.

Piston ring: Hardened metal ring which is a spring fit in a groove running round the *piston* to ensure a close fit to the *cylinder* wall.

Positive earth: The opposite of *negative earth.*

Propeller shaft: The shaft which transmits the drive from the *gearbox* to the rear axle in front engine/rear wheel drive cars.

Pushrod: A rod which is moved up and down by the rotary motion of the *camshaft* and operates the *rocker arm* in an OHV engine.

Q

Quarter light: A triangular window often mounted in the front door of a car.

Quartz-halogen bulb: A bulb with a quartz envelope (instead of glass) and a tungsten filament, and filled with one of the halogen group of gases (often iodine).

R

Rack and pinion: Simplest form of steering mechanism which uses a *pinion* gear to move a toothed rack.

Radial ply tyre: A tyre in which the tread plies are arranged laterally, at right angles to the circumferential plane.

Radiator: Cooling device, situated in an air flow and comprising a system of fine tubes and fins for rapid heat dissipation, through which engine coolant is passed.

Radius arms (rods): Locating arms sometimes used with a *live axle* to positively locate it in the fore-and-aft direction.

Recirculating ball steering: A derivation of *worm and nut* steering, where the steering shaft motion is transmitted to the steering linkage by balls running in the groove of a worm gear.

Rev-counter: See *tachometer.*

Rocker arm: A lever which rocks on a central pivot, one end is moved up and down by the *camshaft* action and the other end operates the inlet or exhaust *valve.*

Rotor arm: A rotating arm in the *distributor* which distributes the *HT* spark voltage to the correct *spark plug.*

Running on: A tendency for an engine to keep on running after the ignition has been switched off; it's often caused by a badly maintained engine, or use of an unsuitable grade of fuel.

S

SAE: Society of Automotive Engineers (of America). The SAE classification of oils is well known but, as with *DIN* standards, SAE covers a wide range of measuring output, performance, etc, of motor vehicles.

Safety rim: A special wheel rim shape which prevents a deflated tyre from rolling off the wheel.

Sealed beam: A sealed headlamp unit where the filament is an integral part and cannot be renewed separately. Although much more expensive than separate bulbs, the illumination does not deteriorate due to contamination.

Semi-elliptic spring: A *leaf spring* used for many car rear *suspension* systems.

Semi-trailing arm: A common form of independent rear *suspension* which allows the wheel carrier to be pivoted.

Servo: A device for multiplying the normal effort applied to a control. With a brake servo, this uses the suction created in the engine inlet *manifold* to act on a *diaphragm/pushrod* for additional braking effort; it's attached to the brake *hydraulic master cylinder.*

Shock absorber: A device for damping out the up-and-down movement of a car when the *suspension* hits a bump in the road.

Sonic-idle carburettor: A *carburettor* where the air used for the fuel/air mixture at idle speeds is mixed in a special by-pass tube which increases the pressure drop. The velocity of the mixture increases to above the speed of sound and at the same time it becomes very turbulent which improves the fuel/air atomization.

Spark plug: A device with a ceramic insulator and two electrodes on a common metal body which screws part-way into the engine *combustion chamber.* When the *HT* voltage is applied to the plug terminal, a spark jumps the air-gap at the electrodes.

Squab: Another name for a seat cushion.

Steel-braced tyre: Tyre in which an extra ply containing steel cords is incorporated to give added strength.

Steering arm (knuckle): Short arm on the rear face of the front *stub axle* to which the steering linkage connects.

Steering rack: See *Rack and pinion.*

Stroboscopic light: A light powered from the engine *ignition system* which is used for checking the ignition timing when the engine is running (i.e. dynamically).

Stroke: The total travel of the *piston* in the bore.

Stub axle: A short axle which carries the wheel only.

Sub-frame: A small frame or chassis which carries the *suspension,* and which in turn is connected to the car body.

Sump: The main oil container at the lowest part of an engine.

Suppressor: a device which is used to suppress or damp-out electrical interference caused by the *ignition system,* or *generator,* wiper motor etc.

Suspension: A general term used to describe the links, springs and *dampers* with which the car body is suspended on the wheels.

Swing axle: A *suspension* arm which is pivoted near the centre-line of the car, and which gives the wheel a vertical swinging action about that pivot point.

Synchromesh: A device in a *gearbox* which synchronizes the speed of one gear shaft with another to produce smooth, noiseless engagement of the relative gears.

T

Tachometer: Also known as a rev counter, this indicates the engine speed in revolutions per minute (rpm).

Tappet: A term nowadays widely misused to refer to the adjustable part of the valvegear of an engine. True tappets are found only in the valvegear of older engines.

Thermostat: A device which is sensitive to changes in engine temperature, and opens up an additional path for coolant to flow when the engine has warmed up.

Tie-rod (track rod): A general term for a rod provides location for a component, or between two components (as with steering linkage).

Timing chain: Metal flexible-link chain engaging on sprocket wheels and driving the *camshaft from the crankshaft* in an *OHV* engine.

Timing marks: Marks normally found on the *crankshaft* pulley or *flywheel* and used for setting the ignition firing point with respect to a particular *piston.*

Toe-in/toe-out: The amount by which the front wheels point inwards or outwards, expressed either as an angle or linear measurement.

Top dead centre (tdc): The point at which a piston is **105**

at the top of its stroke.

Torque: The turning effort generated by any rotating part.

Torque converter: A coupling where the driving *torque* is transmitted through oil. At low speeds there is very little transference of torque from the input to the output; as the input shaft speed increases, the direction of fluid flow within a system of vanes alters and torque from the input impeller is transferred to the output turbine. The higher the input speed, the closer the output speed approaches it, until they are virtually the same.

Torsion bar: A spring-steel bar which turns about its own axis, and is used in some independent front *suspension* systems.

Toughened windscreen: A windscreen which will shatter in a particular way to produce blunt-edged fragments or will craze over but remain intact. A zone-toughened windscreen has a zone in front of the driver which crazes into larger parts to reduce the loss of visibility which occurs with toughened windscreens, but is otherwise similar.

Track rod: A rod which connects the steering arms to the steering gear and/or steering idler gear.

Trailing arm: A form of independent *suspension* where the wheel is attached to a swinging arm, and is mounted to the rear of the arm pivot.

Transaxle: A form of combined *gearbox* and axle from which two shafts transmit the drive to the wheels.

Transmission: A general term for a *gearbox*, but very often used as an alternative for a *transaxle*.

Two-stroke (cycle): A common term used to describe the operation of an engine where each downward piston stroke is a power stroke. The fuel/air mixture is ported into the crankcase where it's compressed by the descending *piston* and 'pumped' through another port into the *combustion chamber*. As the piston rises, the mixture is compressed and ignited, which forces the piston down. The burnt gases flow from the exhaust port, but the piston is now compressing a further charge in the crankcase which repeats the cycle. The engine needs careful design to prevent the unburnt and burnt gases from mixing and, although not a feature of the simplest designs, in some versions a rotary or reed *valve* is incorporated to help achieve this.

U

Understeer: A tendency for a car to go straight on when turned into a corner.

Universal joint: A joint that can swivel in any direction whilst at the same time transmitting *torque*. It's commonly used in *propeller shafts* and *driveshafts*, but is not suitable for some applications because the input and output shaft speeds are not the same at all positions of angular rotation. The type in common use is known as a *Hardy-Spicer*, Hooke's or Cardan joint.

Unsprung weight: That part of a car which is not supported by the springs.

Upper cylinder lubricant (UCL): A type of light oil intended to be added to a car's fuel with the object of providing extra lubrication for the *cylinder* walls.

V

Vacuum advance: System of ignition *advance and retard* used in certain *distributors* where the vacuum in the engine intake *manifold* is transmitted to the distributor and acts on a *diaphragm* to alter the ignition timing according to throttle position.

Vacuum gauge: A device which indicates the amount of vacuum or suction in the inlet *manifold*.

Valve: A device which opens or closes to permit or stop gas flow into the engine.

Vee engine: Design in which the *cylinders* of an engine are set in two banks forming a V when viewed from one end. A V8, for example, consists of two such rows of four cylinders each.

Venturi: A streamlined restriction in the *carburettor* throttle bore which causes a low pressure to occur; this sucks fuel into the air stream to form a vapour suitable for combustion.

Viscosity: A term used to describe the resistance of a fluid to flow. When associated with lubricating oil it's given an *SAE* number, 10 being a very light oil and 140 being a very heavy oil.

Voltage regulator: A device which regulates the *generator* output to a predetermined level. For most *alternator* systems this is an integral part of the alternator itself, and therefore mainly applicable to *dynamo* systems. Regulators on later cars also have a device to regulate the charging current as well as the voltage.

W

Wankel engine: A rotary engine originally developed by Felix Wankel which has a triangular shaped rotor in an epitrochoidal housing (approximates in shape to a broad-waisted figure of eight). The engine has never proved popular in production cars in the UK.

Wheel balancing: Adding weights at the rim of a car wheel so that there are no out-of-balance forces.

Wishbone: An A-shaped *suspension* link, pivoted at the base of the A, and carrying a wheel at the apex. Normally mounted in an approximately horizontal plane.

Worm and nut steering: A steering system where the lower end of the steering column has a coarse screw thread on which a nut runs. The nut is attached to a spindle which carries the drop arm which, in turn, moves the steering linkage.

CONVERSION FACTORS

Distance

Inches (in)	× 25.400 =	Millimetres (mm)
Feet (ft)	× 0.305 =	Metres (m)
Miles	× 1.609 =	Kilometres (km)
Millimetres (mm)	× 0.039 =	Inches (in)
Metres (m)	× 3.281 =	Feet (ft)
Kilometres (km)	× 0.621 =	Miles

Capacity

Inches, cubic (cu in/in³)	× 16.387 =	Centimetres, cubic (cc/cm³)
Fluid ounce, imperial (fl oz)	× 35.51 =	Centimetres, cubic (cc/cm³)
Fluid ounce, US (fl oz)	× 29.57 =	Centimetres, cubic (cc/cm³)
Pints, imperial (imp pt)	× 0.568 =	Litres (L)
Quarts, imperial (imp qt)	× 1.1365 =	Litres (L)
Quarts, imperial (imp qt)	× 1.201 =	Quart, US (US qt)
Quarts, US (US qt)	× 0.9463 =	Litres (L)
Quarts, US (US qt)	× 0.8326 =	Quarts, imperial (imp qt)
Gallons, imperial (imp gal)	× 4.546 =	Litres (L)
Gallons, imperial (imp gal)	× 1.201 =	Gallons, US (US gal)
Gallons, US (US gal)	× 3.7853 =	Litres (L)
Gallons, US (US gal)	× 0.8326 =	Gallons, imperial (imp gal)
Centimetres, cubic (cc/cm³)	× 0.061 =	Inches, cubic (cu in/in³)
Centimetres, cubic (cc/cm³)	× 0.02816 =	Fluid ounces, imperial (fl oz)
Centimeters, cubic (cc/cm³)	× 0.03381 =	Fluid ounces, imperial (fl oz)
Litres (L)	× 28.16 =	Fluid ounces, US (fl oz)
Litres (L)	× 33.81 =	Fluid ounces, US (fl oz)
Litres (L)	× 1.760 =	Pints, imperial (imp pt)
Litres (L)	× 0.8799 =	Quarts, imperial (imp qt)
Litres (L)	× 1.0567 =	Quarts, US (US qt)
Litres (L)	× 0.220 =	Gallons, imperial (imp gal)
Litres (L)	× 0.264 =	Gallons, US (US gal)

Pressure

Pounds/sq in (psi/lb/sq in/ lb/in²)	× 0.070 =	Kilogrammes/sq cm (kg/sq cm)
Pounds/sq in (psi/lb/sq in/ lb/in²)	× 0.068 =	Atmospheres (atm)
Kilogrammes sq cm (kg/sq cm)	× 14.223 =	Pounds/sq in (psi/lb/sq in/ lb/in²)
Atmospheres (atm)	× 14.696 =	Pounds/sq in (psi/lb/sq in/ lb/in²)

Torque

Pound - inches (lbf in)	× 0.0115 =	Kilogramme - metres (kgf m)
Pound - inches (lbf in)	× 0.0833 =	Pound - feet (lbf ft)
Pound - feet (lbf ft)	× 12 =	Pound - inches (lbf in)
Pound - feet (lbf ft)	× 0.138 =	Kilogramme - metres (kgf m)
Pound - feet (lbf ft)	× 1.356 =	Newton - metres (Nm)
Kilogramme - metres (kgf m)	× 86.796 =	Pound - inches (lbf in)
Kilogramme - metres (kgf m)	× 7.233 =	Pound - feet (lbf ft)
Newton - metres (Nm)	×. 0.738 =	Pound - feet (lbf ft)
Newton - metres (Nm)	× 0.102 =	Kilogramme - metres (kgf m)

Speed

Miles - hour (mph)	× 1.609 =	Kilometres - hour (kph)
Feet - second	× 0.305 =	Metres - second (m/s)
Kilometres - hour (kph)	× 0.621 =	Miles - hour (mph)
Metres - second (m/s)	× 3.281 =	Feet - second
Metres - second (m/s)	× 3.600 =	Kilometres - hour (kph)

Index

**Printed by
Haynes Publishing Group
Sparkford Yeovil Somerset
England**